Mediating the Transition: Labour Markets in Central and Eastern Europe

Forum Report of the Economic Policy Initiative no. 4

The authors gratefully acknowledge helpful comments from Anders Reutersward, Lorand Ambrus-Lakatos and Mark E Schaffer. Stefan Profit and Randolph Bruno provided excellent research assistance. Martina Lubyova, Christina Lenkova, Rainer Ohliger, György Lázár and especially Natan Elkin (International Labour and Human Rights Department, ILO) are thanked for providing the authors with data and institutional details. The authors would especially like to thank Claudia Keidel for her excellent editorial work in producing the final draft. This work was supported in part by Sonderforschungsbereich 373 of the German Science Foundation.

Mediating the Transition: Labour Markets in Central and Eastern Europe

Forum Report of the Economic Policy Initiative no. 4

Authors:
Tito Boeri
IGIER, Università Bocconi, and CEPR

Michael C Burda
Humboldt-Universität zu Berlin and CEPR

János Köllő
Institute of Economics, Hungarian Academy of Sciences, Budapest

Editors:
Lorand Ambrus-Lakatos
Central European University, Budapest, and CEPR

Mark E Schaffer
Heriot-Watt University

INSTITUTE FOR EASTWEST STUDIES
NEW YORK • PRAGUE • BUDAPEST
KOŠICE • KYIV • BRUSSELS

Centre for Economic Policy Research

The Centre for Economic Policy Research is a network of over 350 Research Fellows, based primarily in European universities. The Centre coordinates its Fellows' research activities and communicates their results to the public and private sectors. CEPR is an entrepreneur, developing research initiatives with the producers, consumers and sponsors of research. Established in 1983, CEPR is a European economics research organization with uniquely wide-ranging scope and activities.

CEPR is a registered educational charity. Institutional (core) finance for the Centre is provided by major grants from the Economic and Social Research Council, under which an ESRC Resource Centre operates within CEPR; the Esmée Fairbairn Charitable Trust; the Bank of England; the European Monetary Institute and the Bank for International Settlements; 21 national central banks and 37 companies. None of these organizations gives prior review to the Centre's publications, nor do they necessarily endorse the views expressed therein.

The Centre is pluralist and non-partisan, bringing economic research to bear on the analysis of medium- and long-run policy questions. CEPR research may include views on policy, but the Executive Committee of the Centre does not give prior review to its publications, and the Centre takes no institutional policy positions. The opinions expressed in this report are those of the authors and not those of the Centre for Economic Policy Research.

90–98 Goswell Road, London EC1V 7DB, UK
Tel: (44 171) 878 2900
Fax: (44 171) 878 2999
Email: cepr@cepr.org

© Economic Policy Initiative, 1998

British Library Cataloguing in Publication Data
A Catalogue record for this book is available from the British Library

ISBN: 1 898128 32 4

Prepared and printed by Keyword Publishing Services.

Institute for EastWest Studies

The role of the Institute for EastWest Studies has remained constant since its founding in 1981: to help build a secure, prosperous, democratic, and integrated Europe. It does this as a transatlantic, multinational public policy network and think tank working to assist those who make policy in Europe, Russia, the Newly Independent States, and the United States. It seeks to overcome the divisive legacies of the twentieth century while creating a new order in Europe in which governments, the private sector, and non-governmental organizations work effectively together. The Institute is a non-profit organization, governed by an international Board of Directors and funded by foundations, corporations and individuals from North America, Europe and Asia.

In 1990, the Institute launched a major long-term cooperative venture in Central Europe, with a mandate to sponsor dialogue and cooperative research aimed towards building more secure relationships within and between the East and the West. Its steadily growing presence in the region includes centres in Prague, Budapest, Kyiv and Brussels, and the Foundation for the Development of the Carpathian Euroregion (FDCE) in Košice. With direct presence in the United States and Central Europe, liaison offices in other countries of the region, and activities conducted in Western Europe as well, the Institute occupies a unique strategic position between East and West.

The Institute's network of political, business and academic associates and its 60 staff in Central Europe and the United States contribute to economic, security and political aspects of IEWS programmes which include: Community Development and Democratic Institutions, European Security, European Integration, and Financial Sector Reform.

Institute for EastWest Studies
700 Broadway, 2nd Floor
New York, NY 10003
USA
Tel: (1 212) 824 4100
Fax: (1 212) 824 4149
Email: iews@iews.org

President: John Edwin Mroz

Contents

List of Tables

List of Figures

Forum Participants

Vytenis Aleskaitis, *Lithuanian Economic Foreign Investment Agency, Vilnius*
Jozsef Bago, *Ministry of Labour, Budapest*
Iskra Beleva, *Bulgarian Academy of Sciences, Sofia*
Vladimir Benacek, *Charles University, Prague*
Emanuela Bertok, *University of Ljubljana*
Tito Boeri, *IGIER, Università Bocconi, and CEPR*
Jorge Braga de Macedo, *Universidade Nova de Lisboa and CEPR*
Sofia Collantes, *EC Delegation in the Republic of Slovenia, Ljubljana*
Daniel Daianu, *Romanian Institute for Free Enterprise, Bucharest*
Vladimir Dejan, *Ministry of Labour, Family and Social Affairs, Ljubljana*
Bogdan Dobrescu, *Ministry of Labour and Social Protection, Bucharest*
Rumen Dobrinsky, *Centre for Economic and Strategic Research, Sofia*
Robert Drobnic, *Ministry of Labour, Family and Social Affairs, Ljubljana*
Georg Fischer, *Commission of the European Communities, Brussels*
Maciej Grabowski, *Gdańsk Institute for Market Economics*
László Halpern, *Institute of Economics, Hungarian Academy of Sciences, Budapest, and CEPR*
Stephen Heintz, *IEWS, Prague*
Andriej Illarionov, *Institute of Economic Analysis, Moscow*
János Köllő, *Institute of Economics, Hungarian Academy of Sciences, Budapest*
Jenö Koltay, *Institute of Economics, Hungarian Academy of Sciences, Budapest*

Matjaz Koman, *University of Ljubljana*
Irena Kure, *Ministry of Finance, Ljubljana*
Iwona Ławniczak-Iwanowska, *IEWS, Warsaw*
Eric Livny, *EERC – Russia Program, Moscow*
Martina Lubyova, *Slovak Academy of Sciences, Bratislava*
Matthias Lucke, *Kiel Institute of World Economics*
Janez Malacic, *University of Ljubljana*
Vanja Markocic, *Ministry of Labour, Family and Social Affairs, Ljubljana*
Brane Misic, *Labour Union, Ljubljana*
Marcchelo Mladenov Djotolov, *XXI Century Foundation, Sofia*
Amir Naqvi, *EC Delegation in the Republic of Slovenia, Ljubljana*
Leopold Oblak, *Kovinoplastika Loz, Ljubljana*
Joan Pearce, *Commission of the European Communities, Brussels*
Constanze Picking, *CEPR*
Janez Prašnikar, *University of Ljubljana and CEPR*
Andrew Rasbash, *Delegation of the European Commission, Budapest*
Anton Rop, *Ministry of Labour, Family and Social Affairs, Ljubljana*
Andrzej Rudka, *IEWS, Warsaw*
Mark E Schaffer, *Heriot-Watt University*
Sasha Slavec
Florentina Stefanescu, *Ministry of Labour and Social Protection, Bucharest*
Theodor Stolojan, *World Bank*
Miron Tegze, *CERGE–EI, Prague*
Jan van Ours, *Tinbergen Institute, Rotterdam, and CEPR*
Katalin Villanyi, *National Bank of Hungary, Budapest*
Paul Wachtel, *IEWS, New York*
Stephen Yeo, *CEPR*
Jerica Zupan-Van Eijk, *Ministry of Finance, Ljubljana*

Foreword

Launched towards the end of 1995 by the Centre for Economic Policy Research and the Institute for EastWest Studies, the Economic Policy Initiative comprises a programme of interrelated activities designed to strengthen and 'multilateralize' the public policy process in the Associated Countries (ACs) and assist their preparation for accession to the EU. The Initiative operates in seven EU Associated countries – Bulgaria, the Czech Republic, Hungary, Poland, Romania, the Slovak Republic, and Slovenia – where local partner institutes coordinate activities within their own country. Additionally, participants from Estonia, Latvia, Lithuania, Russia and Ukraine are involved as observers.

As part of the Initiative, CEPR and IEWS established the Central European Economic Policy Forum. Here decision-makers from the private sector, senior policy-makers and researchers from both Central and Western Europe meet to discuss key economic policy issues and put forward focused recommendations to the governments of the ACs, the EU and its member states. The Forum meets semi-annually and considers the report of an expert working group, who incorporate into their report the comments and recommendations of the Forum participants for publication. The first Forum Report in the series focused on 'Banking Policies in the ACs', following the conference held at the College of Europe, Warsaw, in January 1996. A pamphlet containing its main analysis and recommendations and a single-page summary of the proposals is also available. The second Report is based on the presentations of the Forum on 'Coming to Terms with Accession', held at Université Libre de Bruxelles in June 1996. The third Report, resulting from the Forum held in Budapest on 16/17 November 1996 with the Institute of Economics of the Hungarian Academy of Sciences, focuses on 'Fiscal Policy in Transition'. This, the fourth Report in the series, has evolved from the Forum on 'Labour Market Policy in Transition Economies', held in Portoroz on 14 June 1997 with the Research Center of the Faculty of Economics at the University of Ljubljana.

We gratefully acknowledge financial support for the Initiative provided by the Ford Foundation, the Pew Charitable Trusts and the EU's Phare Programme. Any opinions expressed in this Report are those of the authors and not those of CEPR, IEWS or the funding organizations. Neither CEPR nor IEWS take institutional policy positions. The funding organizations do not give prior review to the publications within the project, nor do they necessarily endorse the views expressed therein. Lastly, we thank various individuals who have contributed to the success of this project: first and foremost, Constanze Picking and Andrzej Rudka for their energy and determination in the management of the Initiative; Janez Prašnikar and his assistants, Emanuela Bertok, Agnesa Kudic and Matjaz Koman at the University of Ljubljana for organizing the Forum; Julia Newcomb for guiding the Report through production; Iwona Ławniczak-Iwanowska for secretarial assistance in the administration of the project; and last, but not least, the authors and editors, whose effort and cooperation in working under a very tight time schedule has been vital.

John Edwin Mroz
Richard Portes
1 January 1998

1
Challenges Facing Labour Markets of Central and Eastern Europe

The end of communism in Central and Eastern European countries signified not only a departure from central planning, but also the 'return to Europe'.[1] In the first instance, this meant a resumption of a cultural and historical trajectory shared, until the events of the Second World War, by nations ranging from the Atlantic Ocean to the foothills of the Urals. Equally significantly, it implies the beginning of a long process of economic integration, in which trade in goods and services, migration, capital mobility as well as official grants and private transfers once again inexorably link the economic fortunes of these countries to those of continental Europe. This fate is hardly a gloomy one: over the past four decades, Western Europe has enjoyed secularly rising living standards, declining work hours and lower retirement ages, political stability, and most importantly, a peaceful coexistence of nations with distinctly different histories and cultures.

The return to Europe has had a dark side for the economies of Central and Eastern Europe (CEE): it has meant a spectacular rise in unemployment. As if Marx had ordered it personally to prove his point, a 'reserve army' of the jobless emerged in fewer than three years after the fall of the Iron Curtain, comprising 10% of the labour force based on ILO definitions: that is to say, roughly one tenth of those who are willing and available to work under current conditions do not have a job.[2] Considering that communist Europe began the transformation with virtually zero unemployment, it is worth asking, what happened? What is the nature of transitional unemployment? Which policies can best tackle it?

This monograph is concerned with the nature of unemployment in the CEE countries and policies dealing with it. In this first chapter, we

1

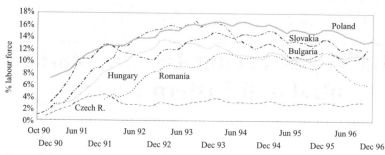

Figure 1.1 Unemployment in CEE. *Source*: National Labour Force Surveys.

characterize the specific features of labour markets in economies in transition. In the second and third chapters, we examine the determinants of labour supply and demand in order to predict where market equilibrium should be in these economies. In the final chapter, we investigate the most important policy issues related to the unemployment crisis in CEE.

1.1   What Happened?

For all its faults and inefficiencies, state socialism did provide a regime of full employment in countries in which it was practised. Perpetually high demand for labour guaranteed a job to every individual who wanted work. Firms were able to finance new employment with cheap credit; the scarcity of materials made it advantageous to have surplus labour on hand when deliveries arrived. Labour hoarding was a fact of socialist life. Central planners evidently attached social value to employment which was greater than labour's marginal contribution to the production process – this was manifested in their willingness to finance inefficient jobs, to bail out bankrupt enterprises, or put administrative constraints on mass dismissals. The workplace was a mechanism of social integration and protection, as well as of redistribution of national output, providing individuals with pecuniary benefits (wages) and in-kind goods and services (medical services, supplementary access to goods in factory stores, vacation homes, child care), in a way that was largely unrelated to individual productivity.

This emphasis on full employment had large efficiency costs. Wages – relative as well as absolute – did not reflect labour scarcity. Real wages were low and pay structures remarkably egalitarian. Wages were much more flexible than in capitalist economies, since workers' paycheques were not necessarily convertible into immediate consumption, but were often saved and earmarked for durable goods with five to ten years delivery time. Under the old system, full employment was imposed on labour market participants, so that there was little or no choice of labour participation, especially since inactivity was stigmatized or downright illegal.

1.2   The Consequences of the Transformation

Full employment was not sustainable as a market equilibrium. In product markets, output collapsed for both supply and demand-related reasons. First, aggregate supply fell as firms lost old clients and had difficulties establishing new ones.[3] Output was homogeneous, input and output channels were not only well established but difficult to change; competition was weak in most markets, and in some non-existent. Firms suddenly had to think about quality, costs, competition, or even simply finding customers. New systems of input supply and marketing had to be established. At the same time, plant and equipment were scrapped and good workers began to look for better options. On the demand side, demand shifted towards Western goods and imports grew steadily, while overall spending fell as uncertainty increased, firms postponed investment projects, and the state began to reduce its role in the economy.

The corollary of developments in product markets was a dramatic decline in the demand for labour. Enterprises began shedding unwanted overhead and excess production labour, first by attrition, later by mass layoffs and plant closures as firms faced an increasingly binding profit constraint. While workers could buy goods with their wages, they could no longer bank on their jobs as certain sources of income. Labour supply also declined over time, as more and more workers withdrew from the labour force. Increases in the effective cost of nursery care and labour supply reducing policies made it more attractive or defensible to stay home, raise children, till the garden, or grow crops for own consumption.

The most striking common aspect of the transformation in CEE labour markets was a dramatic decline in employment rates; that is, the fraction of the working-age population in work. This decline has been as significant in countries where unemployment has risen dramatically, as in those in which it has not, so an explanation of the differences in the rise in unemployment must also be related to labour supply. Labour supply has declined precipitously in these countries to levels comparable with or below labour force participation in OECD Europe. Significantly, this overshooting has affected males more severely than females, leading to higher relative participation rates for females in comparison to other OECD countries.

Reductions in labour force participation have been costly. The actual retirement age has fallen significantly below the statutory retirement age, which is already low by OECD standards. Inherited retirement provisions made it attractive for those with depreciated human capital stocks to retire, and working pensioners were the first to be dismissed. Often, early retirement was justified as a means of getting youth unemployment under control by increasing demand for young workers. As a result of these developments, systemic dependency ratios in CEE countries have risen sharply above levels observed in OECD countries.

This rise in dependency ratios has had significant fiscal ramifications. First, it has led to bloated social security budgets, which by default has led to a rising tax burden on paid employment. Second, the resulting higher taxes on labour have stimulated the informal or underground economy. Tax evasion in this fashion has further contributed to budget problems by siphoning off state revenues and necessitating further increases in labour taxes. The emergence of a 'fiscal trap' is now recognized as an important risk in CEE economies. Excessive reliance on payroll taxes has helped made labour much more expensive than it should be, given local standards of living and labour productivity.

Perhaps in part because of these fiscal traps, the recent recovery of economic output, which in some countries has exceeded expectations, has not resulted in much employment growth. Table 1.1 documents this 'jobless growth' in six of the countries examined most intensively in the study.

1.3   Still Different?

Overall, the scissors of supply and demand help us in sorting out many of the details, but they cannot achieve everything. The transition is clearly a special case. This report has as one of its goals to make this as clear as

Table 1.1   Growth and employment in CEE economies

Country	Time period	Real GDP growth (%)	Employment growth (%)	Employment elasticity of growth
Czech Republic	1993–1996	12.0	−1.1	−0.1
Hungary	1993–1996	5.0	−5.0	−1.0
Poland	1992–1996	22.7	−1.7	−0.1
Romania	1994–1996	17.4	0.0	0.0
Slovakia	1993–1996	19.4	6.0	0.3
Slovenia	1993–1996	12.4	3.4	0.3

Sources: OECD-CCET Labour Market Database and Short-Term Economic Indicators for Central and Eastern Europe, various issues.

possible. Despite the introduction of the market system, labour markets in the CEE countries will continue to behave differently from labour markets in OECD for a number of reasons.

First, a series of exogenous factors, ranging from the collapse of the Soviet Union to inherited fiscal and balance-of-payment problems to wars in the Gulf region and the Balkans, contributed to the 'transformation recession' and continues to influence the recovery of labour demand. All analyses of job growth must be conditioned on these exogenous events. This is especially true for Bulgaria, which was adversely affected by all of these factors.

Second, job destruction and job creation are linked by fiscal policy and the policy regime. Several models have analysed the transition process in this fashion, by focusing on *endogenous* feedback from job destruction to job creation. In particular, fiscal interactions can induce a high unemployment trap and slow recovery from the initial shock.[4] In theory, the state sector sheds labour slowly while the private sector hires either from the unemployment pool, or more likely, from the stock of employed individuals. Higher unemployment tends to moderate wage demands, but also reduces net tax revenues. Slow job destruction will reduce job creation because the wage effect of unemployment is weaker; but it will put less strain on the government budget. Rapid job destruction brought about by aggressive plant closures may bring about more job creation but worsens the government budget balance, leading to higher payroll taxes, lower profitability, less job creation and more activity in the informal economy. There is an optimal speed of job destruction compatible with successful restructuring. For similar reasons, unemployment benefits can also affect the restructuring process: the higher are benefits, the weaker the effect of unemployment on wages, the less restructuring there is, and so on.[5]

Third, newly emerging institutions and behavioural patterns will have an important influence on the dynamics of labour demand. This is true even when one abstracts from factors inherent in the state-socialist legacy or the nature of the transition process. At least a part of the lasting crisis of CEE labour markets may result from factors shaping labour demand during or after 'normal' business cycle recessions in market economies. This is increasingly true as CEE countries adopt institutions imported from the EU. The persistence of shocks has become a central issue in contemporary labour economics, mostly in Western Europe, and will be important element of the discussion of labour market policy in Chapter 4.[6]

1.4   Why Study Labour Markets in these Countries?

There are a number of important reasons for analysing the labour market experiences of CEE economies. Long-term unemployment is high – roughly 50–60% in most countries, and outflows to employment remain low. An unusually large fraction of these individuals are young people. Outflows from unemployment tend to be dominated by exits from the labour force. Large cuts in benefits have only accelerated this trend, but have not themselves led to significant job creation. At the same time, given the structure of non-employment subsidies, there are apparent problems with incentives for taking low-paid work.

As economic growth resumes, there is a risk of a jobless recovery, as has been feared in the United States and European countries of late. Vacancies are low; firms are not yet hiring on a wide scale in the formal economy; given the compressed wage structure, notably in the Czech and Slovak Republics, some of the lack of job vacancies may be related to excessive wage costs in low paid occupations. Even if employment growth comes later, it will leave economic political scars as the expectations of many will be unfulfilled.

Finally, the problem of tax collection and rule of law will accompany, and determine the success of, the transition. Although the underground economy may appear to be Pareto-improving, this assessment neglects feedbacks to the fiscal side; to cover shortfalls, governments tend to raise taxes rather than cut spending. The resulting additional distortions are of first order in magnitude and can be associated with further losses in employment. An important theme of this monograph is the interaction between labour taxes, the underground economy and the social support system, and how this interaction can lead to multiple equilibrium situations, i.e. to different outcomes in identical economies.

The overall impact of association and ultimate accession of CEE economies to the European Union is hard to predict because the labour market will be affected through a number of different channels. The paper touches upon some of these channels without giving an overall final evaluation, which would certainly be premature at this stage. First, accession implies structural adjustment and institutional change. As discussed in Chapter 4, the ambiguous impact on employment and unemployment during the Southern and Northern enlargement of the EU calls for caution with respect to overly optimistic forecasts. Second, in an environment of legal harmonization with continuing political and improving fiscal stability, low labour costs may prove an increasingly attractive aspect for Western investors, with a beneficial impact on CEE labour markets. The hope is that this effect will dominate East–West migration, which will continue unabated as long as the wage gap persists and EU immigration· policies remain fragmented. Finally, a deeper integration with Europe will necessitate the enforcement of EU-conforming regulations in the small firm sector and the (now) informal economy of Central and East European countries, with a possibly adverse short-run impact on labour demand.

Notes

1. The 'return to Europe' is a theme stressed by Sachs (1993).
2. There are some qualifications to this broad generalization, but overall only the Czech Republic has avoided a significant rise in unemployment to date – a case worth examining more closely, as we do below. The external crisis of the first half of 1997 and resulting fiscal austerity will certainly pose a challenge to the sustainability of the 'Czech employment miracle'.
3. See Atkenson and Kehoe (1993), the essays in the Siebert (1993) (especially Hinds, 1993), Brixiova (1995), and Boeri and Oliveira-Martins (1997).
4. See Aghion and Blanchard (1994), Burda (1993), and Chadha and Coricelli (1994).
5. Freeman (1994) and Dewatripont and Roland (1992) focus on the dynamics of *political support* for the reforms and come to similar conclusions: a restructuring process which is too rapid (without compensation for the losers) tends to slow down the pace of reforms. Castanheira and Roland (1996) emphasize the feedback through consumption–savings decisions, arguing that an excessive speed of closure of state sector firms may result in suboptimally slow growth of the private sector via a strong income effect and fall in savings.
6. A number of competing explanations has emerged focusing on the wage pressure of short-term versus long-term unemployment (Layard and Nickell, 1987); asymmetry of adjustment costs in slumps and booms (Nickell, 1995) or insider power in wage setting (Carruth and Oswald, 1987, Blanchard and Summers, 1992) to mention a few.

2
Labour Supply

The sustainability of the present economic recovery throughout Central and Eastern Europe and a successful integration of these countries into the European Union will hinge on the right incentives to induce able-bodied individuals to work, invest in human capital, and match their skills and qualifications with those demanded by firms. It is also important that jobseekers are ready to move where job opportunities are located and compete for jobs with the insiders, if necessary by under-bidding wages paid to the incumbent workers.

Major changes have occurred in the extent and composition of labour supply in CEE. While the focus of the literature has been on the rise and characteristics of unemployment, much less attention has been devoted to those who have left the labour force altogether. However, declines in employment have been accompanied by large flows of persons of working age into inactivity. How strong is the attachment to the labour market of those able-bodied individuals out-of-work throughout CEE? How elastic is labour supply in CEE to new employment opportunities, increasing wage differentials and changes in social benefits *vis-à-vis* income from work? Put it another way: what is the size of *effective* labour supply in these countries?

Data limitations and the still-evolving history of the current economic recovery do not allow clear answers to all the above questions. More modestly, the purpose of this chapter is to shed some light on the changing profile of labour supply in the CEE countries, its composition and likely responsiveness to changing environments. Section 2.1 analyses the decline in employment rates in these countries and the timing and characteristics of flows to inactivity. In Section 2.2 the focus is on those compositional factors that – by reducing the employability of those out-of-work – are likely to make the reabsorption of the unemployed into jobs more difficult in the years to come.

2.1   The Decline in Participation

Employment–population ratios provide a good measure of the degree of utilization of labour resources, and hence of the supply of labour potentially available for the economic recovery.[1] An additional reason for focusing on employment (rather than on labour force participation rates) in Central and Eastern Europe is that in most of these countries open unemployment was rare at the outset of the transitions. Two exceptions were Hungary and the former Yugoslav republics, where not only was unemployment not socially stigmatized, but also some embryonic public income support schemes for jobless people were in place.[2] In other words, at the start of transition, employment and labour force participation rates virtually coincided.

It is widely acknowledged that the CEE countries inherited an inefficient allocation of labour and that most state enterprises were overmanned.[3] A common prediction made at the start of transition was that the imposition of hard budget constraints on enterprises, the shift of workers across firms, industries and occupations, the privatization process, as well as voluntary decisions to withdraw from the world of work (e.g., because work was no longer obligatory and the provision of social benefits was 'detached' from enterprises) would result in declines in employment–population ratios.

Yet, the employment losses that occurred in this process were significantly underestimated. Figure 2.1 documents the rapid decline in employment rates (employment in working age over the working age population observed in all of these countries since the start of the transitions in the late 1980s).[4] The decline is most marked for women, whose participation rates were significantly above those of the OECD countries at the start of the transition in the region, but sizeable also for men, who had employment rates at the beginning of the 1990s comparable to those of many Western countries. Gender differentials in employment rates remain smaller than in many OECD countries. This may actually turn out to be an important advantage of these countries compared with OECD countries that have only gradually closed the gap between male and female participation.

In addition to the sectoral and occupational profile of employment losses – which have disproportionately hit female-dominated industries and jobs in some countries – the decline in female employment rates would seem to be attributable to increasing costs of child-care facilities and policies encouraging women to leave the labour market.[5] Limited part-time employment opportunities are frequently blamed for the dramatic fall in female participation rates. However, part-time employment has rapidly increased in these countries and has reached more than 10% of employment in Poland, a higher share than in some Western European countries (e.g., Italy and Spain). Moreover, many of those working part-time are looking for full-time positions: almost 50% of part-timers were under-employed in Bulgaria in 1996, and roughly 30% in Hungary and Slovakia. In Romania, involuntary part-time work has recently declined from its peak in 1995, where it involved more than 70% of part-time workers.

Another important fact highlighted by Figure 2.1 is that employment rates, notably among males, were already declining *before* the start of transitions. This is partly due to reforms in many of these countries in the second half of the 1980s as well as to the reduced attractiveness of jobs in state enterprises and a flourishing informal sector.

It is often argued that employment statistics in these countries are biased downwards because of the presence of a large unrecorded under-

(a)

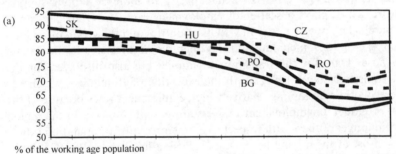

% of the working age population
1980 1981 1982 1983 1984 1985 1986 1987 1988 1989 1990 1991 1992 1993 1994 1995 1996

(b)

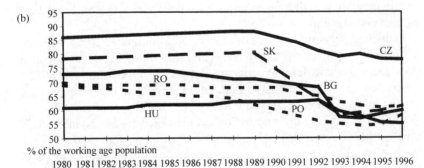

% of the working age population
1980 1981 1982 1983 1984 1985 1986 1987 1988 1989 1990 1991 1992 1993 1994 1995 1996

Figure 2.1 Employment rates; (a) male and (b) female

ground, or informal, economy. While this effect was certainly important for the statistics of the pre-transition period (which were based on censuses of *enterprises*), it is probably less important for the most recent *household* survey-based statistics.[6] The mere presence of a large unrecorded segment of the economy may have resulted in *understating* job destruction in transition, since employment at the start was estimated using enterprise data rather than labour force surveys. Put another way, the trends highlighted in Figure 2.1 might be even steeper if proper account was made of the informal sector.[7]

Table 2.1 provides details on employment rates by age and gender in 1996 and their variation with respect to pre-transition levels. Employment rates declined most markedly at the two extremes of the age distribution. For young people, this is reflected in high youth unemployment rates in all countries except the Czech Republic. Older workers who were laid off mostly withdrew from the labour force either because they took advantage of early retirement or other open-ended income-support schemes, or because they are discouraged workers.[8]

How do the CEE countries compare with economies at similar stages of development in terms of their capacity to mobilize labour supply? Figure 2.2 displays a scatter of employment rates vs. GDP per capita at purchasing-power-parity in OECD countries and the group of middle-income countries, including all the Visegrad countries plus Romania and Bulgaria. Data for the transition economies are also displayed for the pre-transition stage (1989). With the exception of Romania – which has succeeded in maintaining relatively high employment rates because of the size of hidden unemployment in agriculture – all countries in the region are no longer outliers with respect to their employment/population ratios, with most of them lying below the regression line fitting the 1994 data.[9] When account is made of the fact that overall participation is increasing throughout the OECD area, CEE countries have *overshot* the decline in employment–population ratios implied for countries with similar levels of income elsewhere in the world.[10]

Reductions in employment rates can be accommodated either by pushing people into inactivity or by increasing the size of the unemployment pool. Demographic developments, e.g. inflows of large cohorts of jobless youngsters in the working-age population, may also contribute to the decline in employment population ratios. Letting E denote employment, WAPOP the working-age population (women aged 15–54 and men 15–59 unless otherwise specified), U the stock of unemployment, and OLF the stock of working-age persons out of the labour force (without employment and not looking for jobs or not available to work), we can decompose the decline in employment rates as:[11]

Table 2.1 Employment rates in CEE[a,b] (1996 unless otherwise specified)

	Total	Male	Female
Bulgaria[c]			
15–24	19.9	20.2	19.5
25–49	74.8	77.2	72.5
50–54/59[d]	65.4	65.4	69.9
Total	59.5	60.5	58.4
Czech Republic[e]			
15–24	42.5	50.6	34.0
25–49	87.5	93.0	81.1
50–54/59	82.1	83.5	79.8
Total	74.5	80.6	67.8
Hungary[f]			
15–24	25.4	27.5	23.3
25–54	69.0	75.8	62.5
55/59	28.6	43.5	16.5
Total	54.4	60.6	48.5
Poland[e]			
15–24	20.8	22.9	18.7
25–49	74.0	80.1	67.8
50–54/59	49.7	52.5	46.0
Total	56.5	60.7	52.1
Romania[g]			
15–24	42.4	48.9	35.7
25–49	83.9	90.8	77.0
50–54/59	83.7	80.6	89.6
Total	71.9	77.2	65.9
Slovak Republic[h]			
15–24	35.5	38.8	32.1
25–49	80.8	87.7	73.9
50–54/59	69.6	72.3	64.3
Total	66.8	72.1	61.1
Portugal (1995)			
15–24	33.4	38.3	32.4
25–49	79.5	89.1	70.9
50–54/59	73.8	73.6	62.0
Total	64.8	73.2	57.1
Turkey (1995)			
15–24	34.6	39.1	30.4
25–49	61.4	89.4	32.8
50–54/59	54.9	69.3	30.7
Total	53.1	75.6	31.9

Notes:
[a] Data used to calculate employment rates refer to labour force surveys. LFS employment data refer to the first quarter of each year.
[b] Older age group refers to women 50–54 years of age and men 50–59 years of age, unless otherwise defined.
[c] Working age population data include persons 15–54 for women and 15–59 for men, unless otherwise noted.
[d] Youth age group for 1985 and 1992 refer to persons aged 16–24.
[e] Working age population data are held constant from 1995.
[f] The age group 50–54/59 includes men and women from 55–59 years of age.
[g] Data refer to 1995; working age population data for 1995 are held constant from 1993: for 1995 older age group working age population data refer to persons 50 to 54/59, while the employment data refer to persons aged 50–56/61 (women/men).
[h] Working age population data are held constant from 1994.

Sources:
OECD-CCET Labour Market database; Kux (1995), OECD Population Database; OECD Labour Force Statistics, national statistical yearbooks; ILO Yearbook of Labour Statistics.

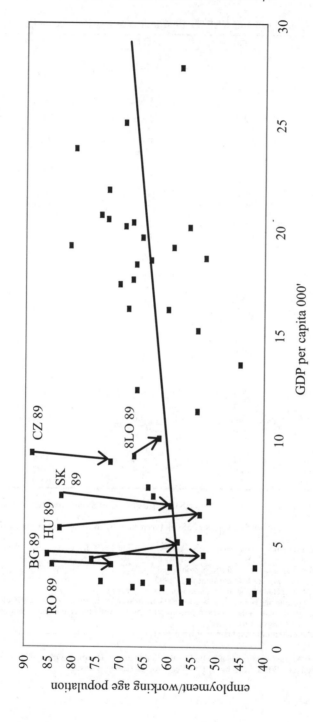

Figure 2.2 Employment–population ratios (a) and GDP per capita (b): international comparisons (1994). (a) Employment over population aged 15–64.

$$-\Delta\left(\frac{E}{WAPOP}\right) \approx \frac{\Delta U}{WAPOP} + \frac{\Delta OLF}{WAPOP} - \frac{\Delta WAPOP}{WAPOP}(1-e) \quad (1)$$

$$\approx \Delta u + \Delta olf - \Delta wapop \cdot (1-e)$$

where small letters denote *fractions of the total working-age population*. In words, the decomposition isolates the amount of dis-employment which has resulted in unemployment as opposed to changes in participation (second term) as well as the role played by demographic developments (third term). Table 2.2 displays the results of the decomposition. In the most egregious cases, dramatic declines in employment were achieved via a rise of inactive population rather than unemployment. The increase in the inactive population in working age accounted in Bulgaria, Hungary and the Czech and Slovak Republics for more than 50% of the decline in employment–population ratios. As expected, demographic factors played a marginal role in the dis-employment process and actually counteracted in most countries the effects on employment–population ratios of the decline in the number of jobs.

Hence, the dis-employment process involved not only the build-up of large pools of unemployed jobseekers, but also an outflow of able-bodied individuals from the labour force. Evidence from matched records (tracking the same individuals over time) across contiguous Labour Force Survey (LFS) waves indicates that large flows from employment to inactivity have indeed occurred.[12] Whilst at early stages of transition, workers were directly moving from employment to inactivity, in the most recent years flows from employment to inactivity increasingly involved intervening unemployment spells (Boeri, 1997b). This is consistent with easier access to open-ended 'out-of-work' subsidies (early retirements, disability benefits, etc.) at the outset and the spread of long-term unemployment (and associated discouraged workers effects) in more recent years.

Economic theory predicts that the choice of unemployed between continuing job search or withdrawing from the labour force depends on the

Table 2.2 Decomposition of the decline in employment rates

		(1989–96; percentage values)			
	Δ(e/wap)	Δu/wap	Δolf/wap	demographic	Δolf/dv
Bulgaria	−22.2	9.9	10.5	1.8	107
Czech Republic	−9.6	2.6	8.0	−1.0	307
Hungary	−22.9	6.9	16.7	−0.7	242
Poland	−13.1	9.4	4.6	−1.0	49
Romania	−5.6	6.3	0.9	−1.5	15
Slovak Republic	−11.6	8.4	4.7	−1.6	56

Notes:
See the text for details on the methodology.
Sources:
OECD-CCET Database and National Statistical Yearbooks.

perceived probability of finding a new job and the expected income
stream from this job versus the value of out-of-work benefits available
when not actively searching. The latter is related to the degree of enforcement of work-tests on the part of national public employment service
administrations or local welfare authorities. As documented in Chapter 4,
increasing unemployment and tight fiscal constraints have forced most of
these countries to restrict sharply the generosity of unemployment benefits. Meanwhile, the scope of social assistance of the last resort has been
expanded, while pension reforms – addressing, *inter alia*, access to and
benefits from early retirement – have been postponed. As outflows from
unemployment to employment have continued to be low, large flows
from unemployment to inactivity have occurred in recent years, shifting
the burden of income support from unemployment benefits to other cash
transfer mechanisms.

Policies designed to ease individuals out of labour force participation
have dramatically increased the financial burden of the social security
system to the state. High statutory payroll taxes have encouraged tax
avoidance in the emerging private sector, thereby setting in motion a
vicious circle in which the contribution base declines in tandem with
increasing tax rates on labour.[13]

Table 2.3 shows that systemic dependency ratios (the ratio of pensioners to contributors) have increased steeply in all CEE countries. In
spite of better demographic conditions than in most Western countries
(as shown in Table 2.2, the working age population is still on a rising
trend in some CEE countries), transition economies are already experi-
encing higher systemic dependency ratios than the OECD area as a whole
(whose systemic dependency ratio was of the order of 38% in 1994). In
fact, the *actual* retirement age in CEE has fallen significantly below the
statutory retirement age, which is itself lower than in OECD countries.
Before the start of transition, the gap between actual and statutory retirement age was smaller and there were many working pensioners who have
been subsequently forced to retire. Especially in Poland and Romania,

Table 2.3 Systemic dependency ratios (pensioners as % of contributors)

	1990	1991	1992	1993	1994
Bulgaria	55	65	78	80	84
Czech Republic	42	46	50	51	50
Hungary	47	50	58	66	64
Poland	40	45	49	53	54
Romania	34	38	43	49	58
Slovak Republic	39	45	50	53	55

Source: World Bank database on Pensions in Eastern Europe, 'Social Challenges of
Transition'.

the share of contributors in the working-age population is significantly lower than the employment rate (Andrews and Rashid, 1996), suggesting a sizeable informal sector.

Flows to inactivity originating from unemployment rather than directly from employment tend to place a much lower fiscal burden on the economy than flows to inactivity originating directly from employment. The tightening of unemployment benefit systems and the spread of long-term unemployment have indeed led to many jobless people flowing from unemployment benefits to social assistance schemes. The latter usually offer lower rate of income replacement than unemployment benefits, but are potentially open-ended and – insofar as access is dependent on an assessment of *family* incomes and assets (means-testing) – may discourage job search of other family members. The 'poverty and unemployment trap' problem – when workers face marginal tax rates for work close to 100% – is more relevant for social welfare than for unemployment benefits.[14]

2.2   Job Generation and Effective Labour Supply

As discussed in the introduction, fast economic growth throughout the region in the last three to four years has led only to modest employment growth. At the same time, Chapter 3 shows that economic growth has been associated with significant real wage growth, not only in the low-unemployment Czech Republic, but also in two-digit unemployment countries like Poland, Slovakia and Hungary. Employment security schemes in Western Europe that traditionally strengthen the bargaining position of the insiders versus those out of work do not seem to play a major role in these countries, as employers have been able to shed labour on a large scale and Western investors often praise the flexibility of CEE labour markets. Rather than due to institutional features of CEE labour markets, the low responsiveness of wages to unemployment in transition economies may be due to deficient competition for jobs between insiders and outsiders, thereby preventing unemployment from exerting significant moderating effects on wage growth. Thus, a central issue addressed in the following three sections is, how re-employable are the unemployed in these countries?

2.2.1   *Regional Mismatch and Mobility*

The regional distribution of unemployment and vacancies is heavily unbalanced.[15] Table 2.4 provides details on regional unemployment

Table 2.4 Regional unemployment differentials in Central and Eastern Europe 1991–94 (annual average of monthly data)[a]

	Year	A Unemployment rate national (%)	B Coefficient of variation [e]	C Top to Bottom Unemployment Rate [f]	D Mismatch index [g]
Bulgaria 9 regions	1991	6.7	0.16	1.5	0.19
	1993	16.7	0.25	2.0	0.20
	1995	11.4	0.32	1.9	0.23
Czech Republic[b] 76 regions	1991	2.9	0.42	2.5	0.32
	1993	3.2	0.62	3.9	0.38
	1995	3.0	0.63	6.9	0.35
Hungary 20 regions	1991	4.8	0.76	3.4	0.27
	1993	12.9	0.34	2.4	0.27
	1995	10.8	0.38	2.7	0.25
Poland[c] 49 regions	1991	11.4	0.35	2.8	0.38
	1993	14.9	0.35	2.7	0.33
	1995	15.5	0.36	2.6	0.32
Romania[d] 41 regions	1991	–	–	–	–
	1992	5.3	0.37	2.8	–
	1993	9.3	0.41	2.6	0.41
	1996	6.3	0.44	3.3	–
Slovak Republic 38 regions	1991	7.0	0.29	2.2	0.31
	1993	14.4	0.37	2.9	0.28
	1995	14.0	0.37	2.7	0.32

Notes:

a National unemployment rates and vacancy rates are weighted by the size of the regional labour force, which is derived from reported regional data.

 – Data not available.

b Annual averages except for missing data in February and August 1991.

c 1995 data refer to the period January–June only.

d Romanian unemployment rates were calculated using the same 1993 labour force data. Data on notified vacancies were not available in 1991, 1992 and 1994. 1996 data refer to the end of the year.

e Weighted (by the labour force shares) standard deviation divided by the mean of regional unemployment rates.

f Unemployment rates for the top (bottom) quarter of the labour force by regions were calculated by ordering regions in terms of descending (ascending) unemployment rates; taking regions until the cumulative labour force exceeded one quarter of the total.

g See note 16 for definition.

Sources: Boeri and Scarpetta (1996) for data until 1994 and OECD Regional Labour Market Database for the 1995–96 data.

differentials in CEE and on the mismatch between the spatial distribution of vacancies and jobseekers. Two facts are particularly noticeable. First, whilst marked regional labour market imbalances had to be expected at the start of transition given the concentration in specific regions of leading industries (e.g., mining, armaments, shipbuilding, etc.), agglomeration effects on the development of a service and retail infrastructure, and the collapse of agricultural output, there are few signs that a re-equilibrating mechanism exists which could reduce these regional unemployment disparities. As shown by columns A through C of Table 2.4, all measures of regional unemployment dispersion are on the rise. Only in the case of Hungary do indicators of regional imbalance not increase uniformly over time.[16] Second, the proportion of unemployed located in the regions offering fewer vacancies – which is captured by the mismatch index on the right-hand-side of Table 2.4 – ranges between 20% and 40% in all countries and also not declining over time.[17] Put differently, up to 40% of unemployment in these countries is structural in that its reabsorption may require regional mobility on the part of workers or enterprises.

Measures of regional unemployment differentials cannot be readily compared across countries, as they are affected by the size of regions and the degree to which administrative regions correspond to actual regional labour markets. The measure which comes closest to providing a basis for cross-country comparisons of regional disparities is the top-to-bottom quartile unemployment rate displayed in column C of Table 2.4. In transition economies, this ratio ranges between 2% and 7%, while in the US, Germany and France it is below 2%, and in Spain just above that level. Among OECD countries, only Italy – due to its North–South divide – shows regional disparities comparable to those of CEE countries.[18]

Regional mobility is hampered in these countries by housing shortages, high mobility costs and uncertainty as to the prospect earnings in the new residence.[19] Inter-regional migration declined after the start of transitions and is only partly responsive to unemployment differentials (see Boeri and Scarpetta, 1996); Kertesi and Köllő (1995, 1997), however, observed an increase over time in the responsiveness of wages to local labour market conditions in Hungary.

However, there are indications that short-run migration is increasing, at least in the Czech Republic, and – given the small size of some of these countries – much of the interregional distribution of labour supply can be achieved by commuting flows.[20] The issue is that, due to poor transportation infrastructure, the costs of commuting are sometimes prohibitively high for the unemployed. Figure 2.3 reproduces the results from a survey on the costs of commuting conducted in 3000 Hungarian villages.

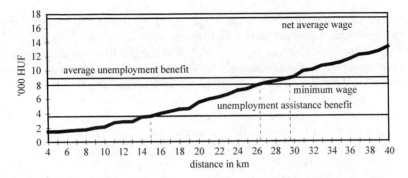

Figure 2.3 Commuting costs, unemployment benefits and income from work, Hungary (1993). *Source*: data drawn from Fazekas, G. Kertesi and J. Köllö, Regional Unemployment in Hungary, Institute of Economics

The average commuting cost between these villages and the closest urban conglomerations is plotted as a function of the distance from the place of work. Commuting costs are estimated in each village by taking the cost of the cheapest means of transportation (e.g., train, bus or car) available to the inhabitants and enabling them to commute daily from the place of residence to the urban area. Information on the average unemployment benefit, the minimum wage and the average wage, net of taxes, in these villages is also plotted in the figure in order to give an idea of the order of magnitudes involved and of potential disincentives to work. The figure points to very high costs of commuting which increase steeply with distance. Commuting costs exceed unemployment assistance benefits just 15 km from the place of residence, reach the level of the minimum wage at about 26 km from home and get larger than the average unemployment benefits only a few kilometres after. Unfortunately, data are unavailable for distances exceeding 40 km, but the slope of the commuting costs line is such that one may guess that the entire salary may be eroded by transportation costs for distances exceeding 50 km from the place of residence. Needless to say, in many Western countries daily commuting takes place at significantly larger radial distances from urban centres. All this suggests that the unemployed in villages offering low employment opportunities but located in a close proximity to buoyant labour markets may find it preferable to stay on the dole rather than commute to the job.

Regional unemployment differentials are also strictly correlated with the spatial distribution of ethnic minorities. Although no reliable data are available on the incidence of unemployment across these groups, several studies (e.g., Uldrichova, 1994; Kertesi, 1994) point to an over-representation of the Sinti and Roma ethnic group in the ranks of the unemployed. It was estimated that in 1993 no more than 30 men and 15 women out of 100 of working age from this ethnic minority were employed which compares with nation-wide employment rates, respectively, of the order of 60% and 50%.[21] The high incidence of unemployment among ethnic minorities originates not only from personal characteristics (e.g., low levels of education) which are not favourable to re-employment, but also from discrimination against these minorities in hiring and firing practices (ILO, 1997).

2.2.2 Characteristics of the Outsiders

Table 2.5 sheds some light on the characteristics of the unemployed and of the hard-core group of the long-term unemployed. Data on the incidence of unemployment are provided for those groups who are most at risk of being unemployed. In particular, the first (second) column display the deviation of the group-specific unemployment (long-term unemployment) rate from the country average, while the third and fourth columns show the share of the group in, respectively, unemployment and long-term unemployment (the set of those with unemployment spells lasting more than one year).

Four facts are important. First, the incidence of unemployment is higher for those who are traditionally most vulnerable to spells of joblessness in Western Europe, especially those with lower levels of education. In Hungary and the Czech Republic, up to 80% of the long-term unemployed have primary or lower levels of education. Second, contrary to what is typically observed in OECD countries, the youngsters are over-represented not only among the unemployed, but also within the ranks of the long-term unemployed. Put another way, youth unemployment is not only a problem of entry jobs, inflated by the entry into the labour market of large cohorts of school-leavers, but a structural issue with pathologies not altogether different than those observed in countries like Italy and Spain. This holds true especially for countries like Slovakia and Poland. Lower shares of young people among the unemployed than among the long-term unemployed suggest, however, that exit-to-job probabilities are still higher for this group than for the older workers. Third, older workers and those above the retirement age are neither over-represented in the stock of unemployment nor are, in absolute terms, a large component of the unemployment pools. Yet it is quite likely that the phasing out of early retirement schemes in most countries will lead to an increase in the share of older workers in the unemployment pools of transition economies. Fourth, there is some

Table 2.5 Characterizing the long-term unemployed (data from national labour force surveys).

	Unemployment rate (deviation from country average)	Long-term unemployment (deviation from country average)	Share in unemployment (%)	Share in long-term unemployment (%)
Female				
Bulgaria	−0.05	−0.06	46.81	46.67
Czech Republic	0.69	0.26	53.01	54.34
Hungary	0.00	0.00	39.11	35.81
Poland	1.46	1.09	51.31	56.25
Romania	0.54	0.47	49.29	42.13
Slovakia	1.33	0.62	50.52	49.92
Slovenia	−0.26	−0.17	44.93	44.44
Youth[a]				
Bulgaria	20.29	8.43	26.92	21.74
Czech Republic	3.30	0.23	29.14	17.92
Hungary	10.91	3.50	26.38	19.71
Poland	16.69	3.21	27.91	19.94
Romania	13.55	4.64	47.81	38.43
Slovakia	9.55	1.92	30.84	22.10
Slovenia	11.17	3.75	31.88	25.00
Older[b]				
Bulgaria	−4.68	−6.27	10.27	4.31
Czech Republic	−1.34	−0.24	9.02	11.56
Hungary	−2.72	−1.04	2.56	2.56
Poland	−5.28	−1.45	7.99	9.67
Romania	−4.79	−2.08	4.00	4.97
Slovakia	−5.17	−1.51	6.04	8.32
Slovenia	−3.93	−2.97	5.80	2.78
Post-retirement age[c]				
Bulgaria	−6.43	n.a.	1.54	n.a.
Czech Republic	0.32	n.a.	5.64	n.a.
Hungary	−3.46	n.a.	0.95	n.a.
Poland	−10.40	n.a.	0.73	n.a.
Romania	−6.69	n.a.	0.41	n.a.
Slovakia	−3.72	n.a.	1.31	n.a.
Slovenia	−7.32	n.a.	0.00	n.a.
Primary or lower education				
Bulgaria	9.13	2.81	45.45	65.28
Czech Republic	5.89	0.58	31.02	86.71
Hungary	6.83	3.20	37.97	77.87
Poland	1.39	−2.52	23.63	27.29
Romania	−1.46	−0.55	28.43	51.94
Slovakia	14.11	0.66	28.45	92.68
Slovenia	3.30	0.62	34.78	66.67

Table 2.5 Characterizing the long-term unemployed (data from national labour force surveys) (contd.)

	Unemployment rate (deviation from country average)	Long-term unemployment (deviation from country average)	Share in unemployment (%)	Share in long-term unemployment (%)
Vocational education				
Bulgaria	−3.04	n.a.	11.10	n.a..
Czech Republic	−0.26	n.a.	42.48	n.a.
Hungary	2.93	n.a.	36.42	n.a.
Poland	3.07	n.a.	43.59	n.a.
Romania	1.63	n.a.	32.10	n.a.
Slovakia	−1.19	n.a.	63.28	n.a.
Slovenia	0.62	n.a.	36.23	n.a.
Unskilled				
Bulgaria	n.a.	n.a.	n.a.	n.a.
Czech Republic	n.a.	n.a.	21.99	26.01
Hungary	n.a.	n.a.	37.48	41.92
Poland	n.a.	n.a.	17.02	17.14
Romania	n.a.	n.a.	8.0	8.00
Slovakia	n.a.	n.a.	18.83	22.08
Slovenia	n.a.	n.a.	8.70	11.11

[a] Persons from 15 to 24 years of age.
[b] Persons from 50 to 54 years of age.
[c] Persons above the official retirement age.

indication that persons with vocational training are very likely to become unemployed and stay on the dole more than unemployed from other groups with some education. This is surprising, as in Western countries the duration of unemployment is typically steeply declining with educational attainment. A possible interpretation for this high incidence of long-term unemployment for qualified workers is in the over-investment made by the previous regime in these training curricula (a point which is further discussed below) and in the specificity of skills taught in these courses which made qualified workers less 'marketable' under conditions of dramatic (and somewhat unpredictable) changes in the skill profile of labour demand.

Long-term unemployment itself is likely to reduce the employability of job-seekers. Estimates of matching functions in CEE (Boeri, 1994b) point to larger elasticities of job finding rates with respect to short-term than long-term unemployment. Moreover, it would seem that in countries like Hungary the current economic recovery is stimulating greater outflows to job rates only for those who have been unemployed for less than one year. Outflows rates to jobs for the long-term unemployed are actually declining over time.

Overall, unemployment pools in these countries are increasingly composed of workers with unfavourable labour market characteristics, such as low levels of education, previous work history in unskilled manual positions and membership in ethnic minorities. Young people also form a large group, but generally have significantly better chances of finding work than other groups. A similar unemployment 'polarization' – with either short or very long unemployment spells – is common to many unemployment OECD countries, and call for labour market policies tailored to the specific needs of each 'hard-core' group. As discussed further in Chapter 4, the need for such policies may be even stronger in transition economies than in the OECD countries as, especially under rapidly changing economic conditions, the fact of being unemployed may convey bad signals to employers and be used as a ranking device in the filling of vacant positions.

2.2.3   Human Capital and Training of the Workforce

The previous discussion suggests that education is increasingly important in determining job finding probabilities, but also that the quality of education matters for re-employment. Despite a near-consensus in the literature that workers in centrally planned economies were well educated and possessed above-average qualifications; in fact, they often over-invested in outdated vocational education with narrow curricula (Flanagan, 1993). It is not surprising that persons with vocational training are currently over-represented in the stocks of unemployment and long-term unemployment.

Another common myth about the legacies of central planning is that the labour force was highly educated. Table 2.6 summarizes available information on educational attainments of the labour force prior to the start of transition in central and eastern Europe compared with OECD countries. This shows that in 1989 far fewer workers had completed general secondary education than in the West. The gap in educational credentials of the workforce is also evident in the case of higher education.

Are education systems in these countries adapting to the changing profile of labour demand? In particular, are they putting a greater emphasis on general secondary education and reducing the excessive role of vocational training under the previous system? Figure 2.4 displays age-specific enrolment rates in the Czech Republic and Hungary as a proportion of those prevailing in OECD countries. While CEE are gradually closing the enrolment gap with OECD countries at all education levels, this gap is still marked at secondary school levels.

Table 2.6 Educational attainment of the workforce at the outset of transition (percent of the labour force)

	Primary or lower	Vocational	Secondary	Higher
Bulgaria	44.6	15.8	30.0	9.6
former CSFR	26.0	21.0	43.8	9.2
Hungary	38.4	23.1	26.9	11.6
Poland	34.2	29.5	27.9	8.4
Romania	35.8	31.4	24.0	8.8
France	35.3	–	46.0	14.6
Netherlands	12.6	–	61.3	19.7
Spain	48.4	–	46.1	5.5

Sources: Boeri and Keese (1994).
General secondary education is 4–5 year programmes allowing pupils to apply for university admission; vocational secondary 1–3 year specialized apprentice schools.

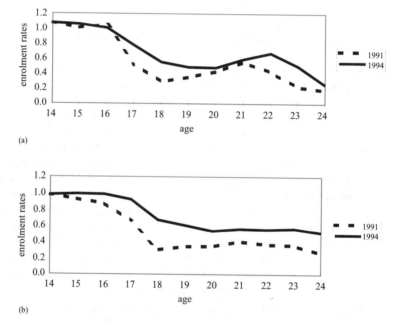

Figure 2.4 Enrolment rates by age in the Czech Republic (a) and in Hungary (b) compared to the OECD average in 1991 and 1994. *Source*: OECD, 'Education at a Glance'. Note: (a) Czech and Slovak republics in 1991

In addition to the levels of secondary schooling, the composition of the education being offered will play a crucial role in the development of fungible skills. A shift of enrolments from vocational schools (and in some countries also technical schools) to general secondary schools has occurred in most countries, just as human capital theory would suggest.[22] In 1994, 30% of the enrolment to secondary education throughout CEE was in vocational schools, down from 36% just four years before. The main exception is the Czech Republic, which maintains a German-style, enterprise-supported vocational training model and where, in any event, the overall secondary enrolment rate has increased.

2.3   Conclusions

Economic transition has been associated with dramatic declines in employment rates. Absurdly high at the outset, CEE employment rates – for males, in particular – have now fallen below those of countries with comparable levels of GDP per capita. Most of those who have left employment are no longer participating in the labour market: they have retired before reaching the statutory retirement age, are simply not searching for jobs, or are engaged in the underground economy. Reductions in labour supply appear even steeper when one considers that a significant proportion of the unemployed has a weak labour market attachment.

Labour slack is also sizeable. There are currently about 4.5 million persons out of work, immediately available and actively searching for jobs, in Bulgaria, Czech Republic, Hungary, Poland, Romania, Slovak Republic and Romania. Another million are discouraged workers and about 600 000 are under-employed, that is, working part-time but are looking for full-time positions. All in all, explicit labour slack accounts for roughly 13% of the labour force or 10% of the population of working age. There are also large reserves of labour in agriculture in Bulgaria and Romania and a sizeable informal sector everywhere. Although many jobs in the informal sector are secondary jobs, it is likely that a large fraction of hidden unemployment would emerge, were opportunities to work in the primary sector offered to these workers.

In spite of this large surplus of labour, strong economic recovery throughout the region is not generating new jobs. This chapter has shed some light on the factors that, by making the outsiders less 'employable' *vis-à-vis* insiders, reduce competition for jobs and hence the moderate effects of unemployment on wages. Regional mismatch of employment opportunities and labour supply is an important factor. In some countries up to 40% of the unemployed cannot find a job without labour (or capital) mobility, long-range migration is obstructed by housing shortages, especially in those areas, mainly the country capitals, where most vacancies are located, and commuting costs are high due to poor infrastructure. The composition of unemployment – with large shares of socio–ethnic groups with a rather weak labour market attachment and many long-term unemployed with low levels of education – is another factor reducing effective labour supply.

The spread of long-term unemployment may also, by itself, reduce exit-to-job probabilities, e.g., because of skill depreciation effects, ranking by the employers on the basis of unemployment duration, decreasing motivation and effectiveness of job search with the duration of unemployment spells, or combinations of all these factors. Although microeconomic evidence on the presence of duration dependence in outflows from unemployment in these countries is inconclusive, recovery seems to have stimulated greater exit from short-term unemployment. Outflows from long-term unemployment are actually declining over time in countries like Hungary, in spite of improvements in overall macroeconomic conditions.

As will be stressed in Chapter 4, public authorities should make it a priority to keep at least a fraction of these people in touch with the labour market, regardless of the explanation for the labour slack in CEE. Current systemic dependency ratios are unsustainable as the increase in the number of pensioners and a shrinking contribution base have put these countries in a worse fiscal situation than most OECD countries, despite more favourable demographic conditions. Moreover, higher employment and labour force participation historically have gone hand-in-hand and there is little doubt that long-term non-inflationary growth is possible by increasing employment rates.

Gradual increases in retirement ages currently envisaged to reduce the fiscal burden on the active population in many countries, will pose new challenges for labour market policies. First, a rising share in the unemployment pool of older people will be difficult to place. Public employment services will have to learn to deal with this new clientele, e.g., by offering support to older people in looking for temporary and part-time jobs. Second, for a given stock of jobs, an increase in the actual retirement age will make the first entry in the labour market more difficult for young people. Rather than continuing to provide the youngsters with unemployment benefits – as done in most CEE countries – a case can be made for encouraging young people to make more productive use of their time before starting their professional careers. Microeconometric evidence (consistent with aggregate data displayed in this chapter) shows that education is the single most important factor affecting employment probabilities. Although the focus of policy-makers has been so far mainly on university education, the evidence suggests that an increase in general secondary education should receive the most attention in these countries. This recommendation will also be elaborated further in Chapter 4.

Notes

1. Statistical and cross-country comparability issues in disentangling unemployment from inactivity reduce the information content of common labour force participation measures.
2. In Hungary, earning-related benefits had been granted since 1986 only to workers involved in collective redundancies, which were, needless to say, a very rare event until 1990. In Slovenia, as in the other former Yugoslav republics, the self-management system allowed compensation to be paid to job losers. The subsidy was administered by the local self-managed units and there were not always sufficient resources to pay all those eligible.
3. See OECD (1993) for a discussion of methodological and statistical problems related to the measurement of labour hoarding in these countries.
4. Given the lower statutory (and actual) retirement ages in these countries than in the OECD average, in Chart 2.1 the working age population is defined as 15–59 for men and 15–54 for women. For the purposes of cross-country comparability, the scatter plot in Chart 2.2 uses instead the internationally agreed definitions, that is, persons aged between 15 and 64.
5. Chase (1995) found that difficult access and increasing costs of child care facilities contribute to explain much of the decline in women participation in the Czech and Slovak lands. Typical is the case of the child-raising support allowance introduced in Hungary in 1993, which was paid *only* to women working *less* than four hours per day.
6. In countries like Italy with a large informal sector, the difference between employment as measured in the labour force survey and employment recorded in census years is often taken as an indicator of the size of the informal sector.
7. See Lacko (1995) for estimates of the size of the informal sector in transition economies. Traditionally employment in the informal sector is combined with regular employment, which means that employment counts *per head* may not be significantly biased. (This is consistent with significant multiple job-holding recorded in labour force surveys.)
8. Data on the discouraged workers (persons without employment, available for work, but not seeking jobs because they deem that there are no employment opportunities or they do not know where to get work) are available only for Bulgaria, Hungary and Poland. In 1996, in Bulgaria discouraged workers accounted for as much as 6% of the labour force, in Hungary for almost 3%, but in Poland for about 1.5%. These proportions are significantly larger than those observed in Western countries (OECD, 1995c) although differences in the design of the LFS questionnaires make such cross-country comparisons somewhat problematic. Like in OECD countries, discouraged workers are concentrated in the older age-groups.
9. Similar results can be obtained by considering labour force participation rates (employment *and* unemployment as a percentage of the population of working age). Kornai (1993) presents a similar chart for the period before the transition.
10. As shown in Chart 2.1, employment rates in CEE had declined even more at earlier stages of transition, which may also point to forms of overshooting in labour market adjustment.
11. In fact: $\Delta(E/WAPOP)_t = (E/WAPOP)_t - (E/WAPOP)_{t-1}$

$$= [(E/WAPOP)_t - E_t/WAPOP_{t-1}] + (E_t - E_{t-1})/WAPOP_{t-1}$$
$$= [WAPOP_{t-1}/WAPOP_t - 1](E_t/WAPOP_{t-1}) + \Delta E_t/WAPOP_{t-1}$$
$$= [WAPOP_{t-1}/WAPOP_t - 1](E_t/WAPOP_{t-1})$$
$$+ (\Delta WAPOP_t - \Delta U_t - \Delta OLF_t)/WAPOP_{t-1}$$
$$\approx n_t(1 - e_t) - \Delta U_t/WAPOP_{t-1} - \Delta OLF_t/WAPOP_{t-1}$$

where n is the rate of growth of the working-age population.
12. Matched records across LFS waves understate actual flows of individuals across labour market states insofar as they rely on discrete time observations of the labour market

states of individuals. This means that if, say, individual A becomes unemployed and then finds a job within the interval between two LFS waves, her/his flow would not be counted. Comparisons of estimated job flows from linked records at quarterly and yearly frequencies suggest that these forms of 'round-tripping' may not be negligible.

13. A key factor determining whether or not this negative scenario will materialize is the capacity of the 'transitional recovery' following the 'transitional recession' to generate jobs and hence bring down (or at least prevent a further rise of) systemic dependency ratios and reduce labour taxation. The role of labour demand is assessed in Chapter 3. Characteristics of labour supply in the CEE countries which may affect the job generation potential of the present recovery are discussed below.

14. See Boeri and Edwards (1996) for estimates of replacement rates before and after exhausting the maximum unemployment benefit duration in central and eastern Europe.

15. This has been pointed out by Burda (1993), Boeri and Scarpetta (1996) and Terrell et al. (1996) among others.

16. In Hungary, the coefficient of variation of regional unemployment rates and the index of mismatch display a somewhat declining trend. A possible explanation for the better performance of Hungary in the reduction of regional unemployment differentials is that there are in this country no national standards for the provision of general social assistance and little redistribution of resources across local communities. Moreover, unemployment assistance benefits offered to the 'exhaustees' are much less generous than elsewhere as they top up the income of the unemployed, not the average income of her/his family. It follows that the unemployment benefit 'exhaustees' in depressed regions have less incentives than elsewhere to stay on the dole (the data displayed in Table 2.4 come from national unemployment registers, the only data providing small-scale representation).

17. The index is defined as follows:

$$I = \frac{1}{2} \sum_r \left| \frac{u_r}{U} - \frac{v_r}{V} \right|$$

where U and V denote, respectively, the total number of unemployed and vacancies in a country, lower case letters denote to regional unemployment and vacancies levels and the subscript 'r' indexes the region.

18. Cf. Boeri and Scarpetta (1996).

19. See Burda (1995) for a discussion of the option value of waiting before changing residence under conditions of uncertainty as to the wages in the new residence.

20. See Erbenova (1995).

21. Cf. Kemeny (1997).

22. This shift from vocational to general secondary schooling was not only supply driven. Often vocational programmes were sponsored, if not provided directly, by state enterprises. When a hard budget constraint was imposed on enterprises, these expenditure items were the first to be cut, while training facilities within the enterprises were divested.

3
Labour Demand

The economies of Central and Eastern Europe lost more than six million jobs during the transition. While roughly a quarter of those who lost their jobs have since left the labour force – many of them willingly – it is uncontroversial that the driving force behind the unemployment problem has been a major and persistent drop in the demand for labour. Changing labour supply behaviour has aggravated this rise in some countries (Poland and Romania), but has mitigated it in others (Czech Republic and Slovakia), while the evidence of the last chapter suggests that further reductions of labour supply are unlikely in the CEE countries.[1] Since labour supply has already dropped dramatically (Chapter 2) progress in reducing unemployment of roughly 4.5 million people in the region is hard to imagine without job creation on a large scale.

The experience so far has been discouraging. Outflow rates from unemployment remain low in CEE economies in comparison with Western Europe, and the recent decline in joblessness is more due to lower inflows rather than higher outflows. This chapter will look at the patterns of job destruction and job creation during the transition and will study prospects for change. The first few sections give an overview of employment during the period immediately following transition. The second part of the chapter then turns to issues relevant for current and prospective evolution of labour demand, especially as regards job creation. In evaluating theoretical sources of sustainable job creation, we are guided by the elementary principle that firms offer jobs up to the point where marginal revenue from an extra employee is equal to wages plus non-wage costs such as hiring or training costs. While cooperatives or other labour-managed firms may deviate from this criterion, the fact remains that the bulk of job creation in CEE countries originates in the private sector. The

overview in the second part of the chapter will therefore focus on factors
shaping the value of a job-worker match, wages, and other costs influen-
cing the supply of vacancies.

3.1 The Transition Shock and its Immediate Aftermath

3.1.1 Labour Shedding before 1989

In two important members of the CEE group – Poland and Hungary –
the transition process began well before 1989, with marked net job
destruction in the state sector. This process can be traced to a massive
voluntary outflow to private businesses and to some early efforts to
reduce overstaffing. In their analysis of 334 Polish state enterprises
over the period 1983–88, Lehmann and Schaffer (1995) found employment declining in the majority of firms and observed roughly the same
rate of job destruction in firms paying below and above estimated marginal products of labour. Similarly, analysing a sample of 2666 medium-
sized and large Hungarian firms over the period 1986–9, Köllő (1997)
observed that employment fell by 17% and labour shedding was only
weakly related to the sales of firms. Analysing about 500 large Hungarian
exporting firms, Körösi (1997) found that mean employment shrank by
21% over the period 1986–9. His cross-section estimates of a labour
demand equation suggested low output elasticities initially, gradually
rising from one-third to three-quarters of the levels estimated during
the transition. Results by Estrin and Svejnar (1996) suggested a similarly
loose pre-transition linkage between output and employment in both
Poland and Hungary.[2]

   The contraction of employment in the pre-transition stage was driven
by two very different motivations. First, it is likely that the outflow to the
emerging private sector was dominated by the most able and ambitious
workers willing to start their own businesses. At the same time, firms
eliminating excess labour had an interest in shedding the *least* productive
workers and benefiting from a reduction in the wage bill with little impact
on output. The observation that labour shedding increased average wages
more than average *residual* wages (that is, wages after controlling for
individual characteristics) hints that the latter effect may have been
stronger, that is, labour shedding was biased against low-productivity
workers.[3] The over-representation of low-skilled, low-wage workers in
unemployment inflow early in the transition period also lends support
to this conjecture.

   In the majority of CEE countries, however, labour shedding started in
earnest only after 1989, as a product of institutional change as well as

supply- and demand-side shocks. While the component of the pre-transition employment decline observed in Hungary or Poland before the transition is hard to identify in other countries, it probably existed to some extent throughout CEE. Accounting explicitly for this component can help explain why changes in employment and unemployment varied so widely among countries hit by GDP cuts of roughly similar magnitude, and why the elasticity of employment with respect to output was lower at the firm level in countries where the introduction of enterprise autonomy coincided with the output shock.[4]

3.1.2   *The Output Shock and its Consequences*

Analysts frequently attribute the adverse labour market developments in many CEE countries, especially Bulgaria and Slovakia, to the 'exceptional severity of the initial shock' (Beleva et al., 1995, p. 228). Not only was the so-called 'transition shock' associated with a massive loss of employment and GDP, but a series of inherited and new problems – ranging from a strongly distorted industrial structure to the adverse implications of the civil war in Yugoslavia – also added to its severity and persistence. Fiscal feedbacks discussed in the introduction only had a modest role at this stage.

The inital sharp rise in unemployment might not be surprising given the exceptional speed of initial job destruction, rising labour costs, high unemployment benefits, a slowly emerging commercial banking system, as well as fiscal imbalance.[5] The first part of the transition period brought unemployment from virtually zero up to a range of 10–15% in Central Europe, 20% in Bulgaria but only 4% in the Czech Republic; there has been little change in the relative ranking since then. Allowing for the case that some new firms appropriated the assets of old enterprises, the evidence lends support to a view of labour market restructuring as a dichotomous process with job destruction in existing firms and job creation (almost exclusively) by new firms. Models approaching the transition problem in this fashion were able to predict correctly the potential for multiple equilibria with high and low unemployment rates.[6] Accepting this hypothesis, the slow rate of job destruction was at least partly responsible for exceptionally low unemployment in the Czech lands, while the rapid rate chosen in Bulgaria is partly to blame for the high rate there.

The Czech Republic is noteworthy in that, in the short run at least, it adopted the right policy mix following the shock and was able to maintain a low steady-state unemployment rate during the initial phase of the transition. First, the pace of job destruction was relatively slow despite the fact that over the period employment rates declined as much as in other countries. This is what indices of inter-industry job reallocation suggest: the Czech gross job destruction rate was 11.6% in 1989–92 as opposed to 15–16% in other countries, while the job creation rate was not much different from other CEE economies. Unemployment inflow rates were also low in the Czech Republic. In 1992, for instance, the average monthly inflow rate was 0.6%, compared with 1.8% in Bulgaria, 1% in Slovakia and Hungary, and 0.7% in Poland.[7] This is due to a large extent to the virtual absence of bankruptcy in the Czech Republic, until recently. Second, large outflows from paid employment (into self-employment) and unemployment (into non-participation) dampened the rise in unemployment. Third, since 1991 the Czech Republic has operated the least generous benefit system in the CEE countries, and has financed it with a relatively intact tax base. Whether this success story will prevail remains the subject of intense speculation.

3.1.3   Flows to Self-employment

In the first three years of transition, total employment fell by 13–16% in Poland, Hungary, Slovenia and Slovakia but only 9% in the Czech Republic and a mere 1% in Romania. These often-cited figures are somewhat misleading, as they hide a major drop in dependent-status employment and a substantial rise in self-employment. Table 3.1 highlights this distinction for six countries.[8]

In terms of employees (dependent status employment), differences between Romania, the Czech Republic and other countries still exist

Table 3.1   GDP, employment, paid employment, self-employment and unemployment – net changes, 1989–92

	Poland	Hungary	Slovakia	Bulgaria	Czech Republic	Romania
GDP (1989 = 100)	82.4	81.8	80.5	71.4	78.9	71.0
Employment (E)	87.4	84.0	86.4	71.3	91.1	98.8
E/GDP	1.06	1.03	1.07	1.00	1.16	1.39
Paid employment (P)	77.1	77.9	80.5	*71.3*	84.3	81.3
P/GDP	0.94	0.95	1.00	*1.00*	1.07	1.15
$\Delta S/\text{-}\Delta P$	0.26	0.21	0.27	n.a.	0.52	0.61
$\Delta U/\text{-}\Delta P$	0.70	0.54	0.59	n.a.	0.20	0.61
Unemployment (U) (%)	14.3	12.6	12.3	15.6	4.3	9.6

S relates to self-employment, U to unemployment.

Source: Employment Observatory, CEC, Bruxelles, December 1993.
The composition of employment is not available for Bulgaria, the figures in italics relate to total employment.

but are not that large. The number of salaried employees fell by 19% in
Romania and 16% in the Czech Republic, in contrast to 20–23% in
Poland, Slovakia and Hungary. In Romania, employment losses in the
enterprise sector were largely offset by a rise of self-employment, primarily in agriculture, but also to a smaller extent in trade and catering.
Unemployment there would have remained low had inflows from non-
participation to unemployment not worked to offset this effect. In the
Czech Republic, both massive inflows to self-employment and flows out
of the labour force kept unemployment low. The net increase of self-
employment absorbed *over half* of the net decrease in paid employment,
compared with about a *quarter* in Poland, Hungary or Slovakia. (By
contrast, the rise in unemployment represented 54–70% of the decline
in paid employment in these countries as opposed to only 20% in Czech
Republic.) The niche to be filled in the Czech Republic was tremendous
given that the share of self-employment in the former Czechoslovakia
was a mere 0.4% in 1989, in contrast to 6.9% in Romania, 7.7% in
Hungary, 9.5% in Slovenia, or 16.6% in Poland.[9] The small privatization
programme facilitated the flow to self-employment in Czech Republic
and helps explain a part of the unemployment gap between the Czech
and Slovak lands. The data in Table 3.1 suggest that the unemployment
rate would have been over 9% in the Czech lands by the end of 1992, had
absorption into self-employment occurred at the same rate as in
Slovakia.[10]

Three conclusions can be drawn from Table 3.1. First, total employment figures *underestimate* the shock to labour demand (in the enterprise
sector), especially in countries where the private sector was small before
1989. Second, the cross-country differences in terms of net job destruction by firms are not as large as one would think on the basis of total
employment figures. Third, it is apparent that flows to self-employment
constituted the first important component of structural change early in
the transition.[11]

3.1.4   Inter-industry Restructuring

Following Davis and Haltiwanger (1993) and applications of their con-
cepts to the CEE economies by Konings et al. (1996) and Mancellari et al.
(1996), we characterize the nature of inter-sectoral job flows starting with
Table 3.2, in which five measures of job reallocation are displayed. The
first measure, *pos*, relates net job creation in expanding sectors to the
mean of employment in the current and previous periods; *neg* measures
job destruction in contracting sectors.[12] By construction, *pos* and *neg* lie
in the interval [0,2]. The gross job turnover rate (*gross*), net job creation

(*net*), and the excess of gross job creation and destruction above that implied by *net* (*excess*)- are defined as: *gross = pos + neg*; *net = pos − neg* and *excess = pos − |net|*.

Table 3.2 presents estimates of these measures for six countries over 11 industries.[13] At the industry level, data for the first stage of transition (typically 1989–92) suggest that restructuring was achieved by the contraction of oversized sectors rather than by the expansion of undersized ones. Döhr and Heilemann (1996) show that the *relative* size of industries moved rapidly towards levels predicted by the Chenery hypothesis during this period.[14] In 1992, the industrial structure was markedly closer to

Table 3.2   Measures of job destruction and job creation (%)

	pos	*neg*	*gross*	*net*	*excess*
Continuing firms					
Poland[a]					
1988	0.7	3.6	4.3	−2.8	1.5
1989	0.2	6.1	8.1	−4.0	4.0
1990	0.6	15.3	15.0	−14.6	1.3
1991	1.0	17.6	18.6	−16.5	2.1
Hungary (cumulative)[b]					
1986–1989	1.1	22.6	23.5	−21.5	2.0
1989–1992	3.5	52.9	56.4	−49.4	7.0
1992–1995	6.3	37.6	43.9	−31.3	12.6
Poland[a]					
state, 1991	1.0	17.6	18.6	−16.5	2.1
private, 1991	9.6	21.6	31.3	−11.9	19.3
Hungary (cumulative)[b]					
small firms, 1992–95	14.6	27.2	41.8	−12.6	29.1
Industries					
Bulgaria[c]					
1989–92	–	–	11.2	–	–
1992–94	–	–	3.1	–	–
Czech Republic[d]					
1989–92	2.6	11.8	14.4	−9.2	5.2
1993–95.2	4.4	2.3	6.7	2.1	4.6
Hungary[d]					
1989–92	–	–	–	–	–
1993–95.2.	1.3	5.7	7.0	−4.0	2.6
Poland[d]					
1989–92	1.4	16.1	17.5	−14.7	2.8
1993-95.2.	3.6	3.1	6.7	0.5	6.2
Romania[d]					
1990–94	6.1	15.1	21.2	−9.0	12.2
1994.1.–95.1.	4.3	2.1	6.4	2.2	4.2
Slovakia[d]					
1989–92	2.1	16.4	18.5	−14.3	4.2
1994–95.2	3.3	1.7	5.0	1.6	3.6

[a]Konings et al. (1996), [b]Author's calculation using NLC Wage Survey Firm Panel Data introduced in Köllő (1997), [c]Mancellari et al. (1996), [d]Authors calculation using data from EC8 (1995).

patterns characteristic of market economies than it was in 1989. Assuming a middle-of-the-period stock of 100, industries with employment growth created 1–2% net employment. In contrast, contracting industries reduced employment substantially, by 11.6% in the Czech Republic and 15–16% in other countries. Romania was exceptional in that its flow to self-employment – characteristic of all reforming countries – also crossed industry frontiers, notably, the one between industry and agriculture. Agricultural employment in Romania increased by 16% in 1990–94, explaining most of the country's 'high' *pos* value of 6.1%. With the exception of Romania, the amount of inter-industry job turnover which accompanied the given net change (shown by *excess*) was also low, falling to a range of 3–5%.

Table 3.3 presents a more detailed view of sector-level changes of employment in absolute terms, for countries and periods covered by comparable statistics. The 'Visegrad 4' followed similar patterns in that employment in the production sector declined substantially and, as far as Poland, Hungary and Slovakia are concerned, by similar orders of magnitude.[15] The decline in these branches was less severe in the Czech Republic. The growth of the tertiary sector was not only insufficient to absorb this decline; in Poland and the Czech Republic, there was little if any growth at all until mid-1992. The rate of growth was negligible in Hungary and Slovakia. Only in Romania do we see a major net shift from industry to tertiary employment (and agriculture).

These data seem inconsistent with the usual story of booming trade and services early in the transition. Excluding the possibility that the data are wrong, at least four factors may be responsible. First, as was mentioned, the data do not cover the most turbulent year of the transition

Table 3.3 Change of employment in the early stages of transition (thousands)

Country:	Czech Republic	Hungary	Poland	Romania	Slovakia
Period:	1989–92	1989–91*	1989–92	1990–92	1989–92
Agriculture	−204	−160	−718	+289	−80
Mining	−73	−27	−119	+13	−1
Manufacture	−257	−97	−516	−748	−178
Power and water	+4	−14	−40	+31	−2
Construction	+6	−35	−255	−127	−70
Transport and comm.	+5	*+15*	−254	−115	−2
Trade and catering	+2	*+95*	+167	+205	−38
Financial services	+6	*+18*	+27	+27	+8
Other services	−78	−62	−232	+10	−12
Health and education	+0	*−23*	−44	+7	+4
Public administration	+1	*−57*	+34	+25	+36

Source: EC8 (1995), pp. 33–37, except Hungary, numbers printed in italics, estimated by the authors from EC1 (1992) and KSH (1993). *By resident population at end 1992.

period. Second, the effect on employment of self-employment may be exaggerated: 20 000 new shops may seem a tremendous change for consumers but the implied employment gain (40 or 50 000 at best) is small. Third, a great deal of gap-filling in trade and services may have implied *intra*-industry labour flows: the takeover of state retail stores and restaurants by people who had run them, farm start-ups by former cooperative members, and so on. Finally, some employment growth in tertiary sectors may be in the informal economy for tax avoidance purposes, and thus are not counted.

3.1.5   Continuing Firms

The data discussed above suggest that some industries were contracting more than others but none of them expanded significantly; most job reallocation has occurred *within* industries, and hence a closer look at the enterprise level is called for.[16] The enterprise-based data in Table 3.2 also suggest extremely low job creation rates (1–3%) in both Poland and Hungary in 1989–92. In contrast, the job destruction rate more than doubled as these countries entered the stage of transition. The Polish figures hint at 15% job destruction by contracting firms annually, while the Hungarian ones suggest a 53% rate over a three-year period. Accordingly, both *gross* and *net* were strongly dominated by job destruction in contracting enterprises, and the level of 'churning' (as measured by *excess*) was relatively small.

While declines in output and employment were more closely correlated at the firm level than before, estimates of elasticity of post-transition employment with respect to output have been low (Estrin and Svejnar, 1996; Köllő, 1996; Commander and Dhar, 1996), although this may not be a good indicator of future firm behaviour. Studies indicate that an overwhelming majority of firms cut employment in the first years of transition even in the emerging private and small firm sectors. In Poland in 1991, Konings et al. (1996) observed net employment destruction even in continuing *private* firms (although no distinction is made between start-up private and privatized enterprises) and even in the period 1992–95 indices for continuing small firms in Hungary show a *net* value of −0.126.

3.1.6   New Firms

It is a common observation of researchers working with enterprise panels that *aggregate* employment fell less steeply than employment in *continuing* firms. This is because a wide gap was filled by new firms and/or employment growth in small enterprises incompletely covered by firm surveys. Unfortunately, data on the nature of firm creation are scarce and unreliable, so little can be added to this general statement at the present.

First, it is difficult to distinguish between firms created 'ab initio' with fresh capital and units detached from large enterprises. The possible size of the bias is well shown by a study by Major and Voszka (1996). The 49 large Hungarian enterprises they followed over the period 1980–93 literally disintegrated into a complex of 366 legal entities by 1989 and 620 by 1993. Considering only cases for which the source of investment is known (215 cases), about two-thirds of the new firms had no outside investor, but simply separated from the master enterprise with assets and workers attached. Accounting such a shift as 'job destruction' in a large firm and 'job creation' in a new firm is not fully consistent with the usual interpretation of these notions.[17]

Second, the figures on firm creation are biased by a high proportion of non-operating firms and ventures aimed at tax fraud, and by outsourcing, or cases in which firms employ workers under the condition that they act as independent contractors.[18] One robust result is that most new jobs were created by newly established business units. Most of these units are *de facto* privately owned and even those detached from state enterprises are typically subject to profit-seeking managerial or owner's control. The almost exclusive role played by new units in job creation provides a good measure of private sector growth (certainly better than the doubtful statistics on the share of 'private' ownership).

3.2   The Maturation of CEE Labour Markets

Since 1993, almost all CEE economies have shown clear signs of recovery from the 'transformational recession'. In Poland, Slovakia and Romania, GDP has grown since 1994 by more than 5% per annum; in the Czech Republic and Hungary, growth has been more modest but none the less positive. At the same time, output growth has failed to imply employment growth of comparable magnitude and in some countries employment continues to decline. The dynamics of self-employment have continued to play a role in the transition, albeit a smaller one. The share of self-employment increased further in Romania and the Czech Republic, and marginally in Slovakia and Hungary. Only Poland was the exception to this trend, due to a continuing 'secular' contraction of agriculture. Apart from Poland and Romania, where private farming on small plots leads to extremely high shares of self-employment in total employment (29.9% and 38.3% in 1995, respectively), we observe a level-ling-off of cross-country differentials. The shares were 11.5% in Bulgaria, 11.6% in Czech Republic, 10.6% in Hungary and 6.5% in Slovakia. This remains true if we exclude agriculture (13.4% in Hungary, 10.2% in Poland, 9.6% in CR and 6.4% in Slovakia).[19] These figures suggest that the niche to be filled is substantially smaller now than it was at the start of transition. Considering that self-employment (as observed in labour force surveys) also includes cases of casual work by jobless people, we might expect that economic recovery could induce a decrease within this category. Taking these two points together, it seems rather unlikely that the former dynamism of job creation, in the form of sole proprietorships, may continue.

Indicators of industry-level job reallocation displayed in Table 3.2 suggest a slowdown of structural change in both absolute and relative terms. The rate of job destruction by contracting industries declined from 12–16% in 1989–92 to 2–3% in 1993–5 everywhere except in Hungary, where it remained at a slightly higher level (5.7%). Job creation by expanding industries increased to 3–4%, except in Hungary where it remained at 1.3% even in the mid-1990s.[20] Both gross and excess measures were far lower in 1993–5 than earlier.

Table 3.4 provides useful information on the sectoral sources of employment growth for the Visegrad countries (delivering comparable

Table 3.4   Change of employment in the later stages of transition (thousands)

Country: Period:	Czech Republic 93–95.2	Hungary 93–95.2	Poland 93–95.2	Romania 94.1–95.1	Slovakia 94–95.2
Agriculture	−55	−57	−417	+240	−16
Mining	−27	−7	+14	+21	−5
Manufacturing	−17	−90	−39	−189	+9
Power and water	+4	−7	+106	+20	−3
Construction	+23	+8	−10	+16	−3
Transport and comm.	−10	−21	+125	+12	+1
Trade and catering	+104	−12	+231	+46	+21
Financial services	+25	+10	−106	+10	+5
Other services	+32	+14	−5	−13	+25
Health and education	−2	−18	+16	−26	−4
Public administration	+18	+18	+38	+111	+10
Total**					
Employment	+96	−163	−4	+238	+35
Employees	−36	−200	+176	−207	+28
Self-employed	+132	+37	−180	+446	+7

Source: EC8 (1995), pp. 33–37. *By resident population at end 1995. ** The figures on total employment and sectoral distribution come from different sources. For that reason, and rounding, the sum of the changes of subtotals may differ from the change of the total. The differences are 1, 7, 21, 10 and 5 thousand, respectively.

information across branches over the period 1993–5). The figures suggest diverse fluctuations in sectoral employment levels. Public administration expanded uniformly in all countries up until the end of 1995, as did most tertiary sectors. Industry declined secularly in Hungary, with no remarkable job creation in other sectors. In the Czech Republic and Slovakia, job creation in the tertiary sector could more than offset the ongoing job destruction of agriculture and, to a smaller extent, of other 'material sectors'. Poland had modest growth in all sectors except agriculture. By contrast, net flow into agriculture remained a distinctive feature of the Romanian labour market.

Information on enterprise behaviour during the later stage of transition remains scarce. Our understanding of the recent unemployment flow figures is that firms fire fewer workers but their hiring rates remain low (Boeri, 1996). There is evidence from Hungarian Labour Force Survey, however, that the outflow rate from short-term unemployment increased in 1994–95 while the rate from long-term unemployment decreased. This suggests that the market may have improved for more 'employable' workers and the overall unemployment outflow rates may underestimate the improvement in job offers. In Hungary, there is new evidence that firms expanding *output* increasingly do so by expanding *employment* (Köllő, 1996) and this holds for large privatized firms as well. Pinto and Wijnbergen (1995) showed, already at early stages of the transition, that some large Polish state firms underwent major restructuring and had good hopes for expansion. In all countries, we find 'dinosaurs' who defied the odds and have prospered; in addition, many of them operate in heavy industry sectors. Statistics, available studies and anecdotal evidence all suggest that the downsizing of large firms and socialist 'priority industries' has stopped.

The character of restructuring also tends to change for reasons related to private sector growth. The early stage of transition, when missing markets in retail and wholesale trade, finance and services provided an opportunity for extraordinary profits for new entrants, is over. The gaps in the consumer markets are being filled and *legislative* barriers to small and medium-sized firms are no longer as severe as at the start of transition.[21]

Judging from CEE-EU comparisons of firm density (Eurostat, 1996), employment growth from expansion of existing units (as opposed to firm creation) seems more plausible at this stage of the transition. In 1995, CEE economies were already close to the European Union average of 43 firms/1000 inhabitants (including sole-proprietorships but excluding agriculture). Firm density exceeded 50 in the Czech Republic and Hungary and 35 in Slovenia, Slovakia and Bulgaria.[22] The proportion of firms without salaried employees, however, still exceeded 60% in all CEE countries (except Slovenia), compared to an EU average of 49.7%. Changing the unbalanced firm size distribution in the enterprise sector will require economic growth, and the resulting transformation of sole proprietorships to small capitalist enterprises on a large scale.

From the above discussion, it follows that the conditions shaping labour demand are becoming less and less 'transition-specific.' Most firms are trading in and producing for competitive markets now, with hard budget constraints and equal treatment, so their expected profit is predominantly affected by relative productivity and costs.[23] When firms create jobs they balance the marginal revenue product from a prospective job-worker match against wages, taxes, and capital costs. If differences across CEE economies exist, they are likely to be found in the level and evolution of these costs and benefits. Therefore, in assessing the conditions of employment growth the following sections will put the emphasis mostly on wages, non-wage charges, and other costs relevant for job creation.

3.3   Current Constraints on Employment Growth in CEE

The employment effect of GDP growth has so far remained modest in CEE countries. There is one compelling reason to regard this jobless recovery as a short-term phenomenon: if structural change means a shift from sectors with low labour productivity towards high productivity units, employment should recover later than output. Economic arguments and the facts lead us to believe, however, that a number of other factors are responsible as well.

First, despite years of downsizing, relative overmanning remains a problem in some former state enterprises. Second, and more relevant, the poor quality and quantity of the inherited capital stock tends to reduce the demand for labour at a given rate of output growth and/or capital formation, and more important, for a given wage level. Third, wage costs themselves, for given size and quality of the capital stock, may also represent a brake on employment growth. Labour costs are determined by direct wages and salaries, non-wage labour expenses, payroll taxes, relative terms of trade of output prices, and a host of other factors. Labour costs may also be influenced by a 'virtual' component which includes the expected costs of severance and recuperation of training and hiring costs, as well as the expectation of future wages.[24] Finally, the presence of foreign firms, which are less likely operate under the previously mentioned three constraints, seem likely to increase employment, all other things equal.

3.3.1   Persistent Overmanning

First, the more firms reduced their inherited excess staff, the more likely they were to hire outside labour in response to positive shocks. The first question is, to what extent have they succeeded, and what can empirical research tell us about it? Basu et al. (1994) conclude, on the basis of labour demand equation estimates for Polish and Czechoslovak firms, that 'even after the reductions in employment in 1990–92 state-owned firms still have a larger stock of labour, *ceteris paribus*, than other types of firms' (p. 12). Almost half of the Polish firms interviewed in 1993 by Brada and Singh (1994) reported that their employment level is 'too high'. This was the case in particular in state firms and joint stock companies (53% and 58% as opposed to 38–39% in private and privatized firms). In Hungary 1994, cooperatives and state firms still shed labour in all categories of sales change (except for cooperatives increasing sales by more than 50%) as shown in Köllő (1996). These figures suggest that although some of the former state firms managed to survive and may even expand, their demand for additional labour is likely to be limited in the short to medium run.

3.3.2   Deficient Capital Stock

The capital stock – measured by its quality and quantity – represents a second important constraint on employment growth. Capital and labour are to some extent complements in production, and a decline in the user cost of capital, or positive externalities due to improvements in infrastructure, may lead to employment growth *induced* by the expansion of the capital stock *per se*; more generally, an expansion of output at given factor prices is possibly only by increasing both labour and capital inputs. Normally, at the end of usual business cycle recessions the condition for complementarity is fulfilled in many firms; when bad times are over, idle plants and machines can be restarted and workers recalled.[25] In the presence of unused but usable capacities, employment can recover faster for that reason. Also, the inflationary and trade-balance risks of demand-side stimuli are lower in this case and their effect on employment can be more long lasting.[26]

As might be expected, the unused capacities of CEE enterprises are generally inadequate for producing goods of standard quality for competitive markets, or can do so only at very low wage levels. The scope for restarting idle plants is limited and the positive feedbacks mentioned above are typically not operative. In order to increase employment, firms must first increase the stock of plant and equipment, which induces slower, more drawn-out adjustment to positive shocks.

To illustrate this, Table 3.5 presents data from a Hungarian firm survey. Firms are grouped by the change in their order book and by physical capital formation (whether they planned to activate new equipment or structures during the year). In 1992, 1993 and 1994 the tables indicate employment growth in firms with increasing orders *and* increasing phys-

Table 3.5 Percentage change of employment in various groups of firms (Hungary, National Labour Centre Forecast Survey 1992, 1993, 1994)

(i) All firms in the samples

Orders over previous year	Type of capacity activated during the year			
	None	Equipment	Building	Both
1992				
less	−8.7	- - - - - - - - - - - - - - - - −4.8 - - - - - - - - - - - - -		
same	−2.3	- - - - - - - - - - - - - - - - −1.0 - - - - - - - - - - - - -		
more	−1.7	- - - - - - - - - - - - - - - - +3.0 - - - - - - - - - - - - -		
1993				
less	−8.0	−9.7	−15.0	−18.0
same	−9.4	−5.4	−7.3	−9.4
more	−4.4	+7.2	+4.5	−4.4
1994				
less	−14.1	−9.9	+1.6	−14.7
same	−5.6	−4.7	−2.3	−1.4
more	+0.1	+6.2	+1.8	+8.5

Number of observations: 1992 = 3905, 1993 = 4178, 1994 = 4517.

(ii) Continuing firms (1992–94)

Orders over previous year	Type of capacity activated during the year			
	None	Equipment	Building	Both
1992				
less	−25.0	−9.5	−9.9	−25.5
same	−16.0	−7.7	−6.7	−1.60
more	−4.9	+18.7	+0.4	−4.9
1993				
less	−19.5	−20.1	−17.6	−19.2
same	−14.6	−9.7	−8.3	−20.1
more	−12.8	−4.7	+11.3	+13.3
1994				
less	−26.3	−32.2	−17.8	−10.6
same	−10.5	−9.3	−5.6	−2.3
more	−3.2	+0.9	+7.1	+18.1

Number of observations: 1115. Firms are weighted by employment at 1 January of the respective year.

ical capital. In other categories (including the case of growing orders but no investment) employment appears to fall. Though this survey is not representative, the coincidence of employment growth and physical capital formation over three consecutive years in a fairly large sample suggests that hiring without adding new physical assets may be unprofitable, given wage levels and the state of the existing technology.

The emphasis on capital formation as a clue to employment growth is not uncontroversial, as the discussion of European unemployment illustrated in the 1980s.[27] High savings and investment are necessary conditions for growth, but long-term effects on unemployment rates are theoretically uncertain. Layard and Nickell (1986) found little evidence of any such connection in Britain; Layard et al. (1991) analysed European unemployment without much emphasis on the issue of the capital stock. Others argue that a rise in the capital stock does induce a rise in employment if (a) real wages are rigid (Burda, 1988a; Bean, 1989), (b) capital and labour are complements (Snower 1995) and (c) capital reduces inflationary pressure and the natural rate of unemployment (Rowthorn 1995). In the case of investment in CEE, a combination of these factors have led to a 'post-war' situation in which these countries lost (once and for all) a huge component of their capital stock and now foresee a period that to some extent resembles a 'reconstruction period' when capital formation does indeed matter.

3.3.3   *Labour Costs*

Wages are relevant for employment during the recovery for several reasons. The importance of real wages and labour costs can be seen for the case of the former Czechoslovakia early in the transition, when they fell steeply. The hourly US dollar compensation cost of production workers in Czech manufacturing decreased by 30% in the Czech Republic in 1989–92, while they increased by 56% in Hungary and 27% in Poland. Unit labour costs (ULC) changed by −15%, +17%, and +22%, respectively. As Blanchard et al. (1995) and Godfrey (1993) have shown, the CPI/PPI wedge had more to do with the divergence of labour costs across countries than with the fall of consumer real wages. The undervalued crown also contributed to favourably low labour costs in dollar terms. The reasons are potentially different from those outlined in 'two-sector' labour market models, but the contribution of falling labour cost to job retention and job creation was certainly positive.

Net consumer real wages declined sharply in all reforming economies (including former outlier Hungary where the bulk of the squeeze came with a delay in 1995–6) but unit labour costs did not follow in all CEE countries. Since dollar ULC are affected by labour productivity, nominal wages, the producer price index, and the exchange rate, its level and path are heavily influenced by the composition of stabilization packages and the timing of reforms. Drawing data from Havlik (1996), Figure 3.1 shows the evolution of exchange-rate-adjusted unit labour costs in 7

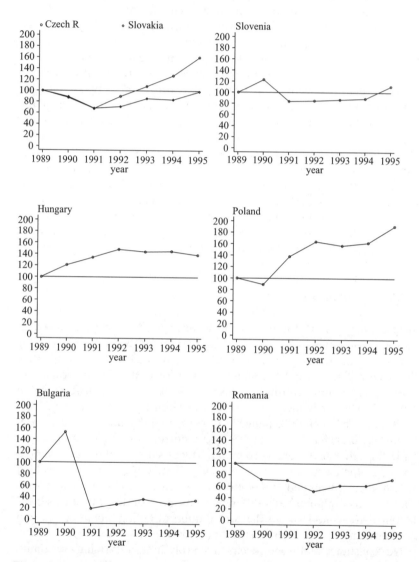

Figure 3.1   Unit labour cost (exchange rate-adjusted, 1989 = 100).
Source: Havlik (1996)

countries over the period 1989–95. In most countries, the initial currency devaluation brought the ULC down below its pre-transition level but following this shock, labour costs showed an increasing trend. In 1995, dollar labour costs were significantly above their 1989 level in Poland, the Czech Republic and Hungary and close to their initial value in Slovenia and Slovakia. Only in Bulgaria and (less so) in Romania was ULC well below the pre-transition level.[28]

Despite a basically increasing trend following the early stabilization period, the *level* of labour costs remain low in European comparison (Havlik, 1996), even compared to Mexico or the South Asian 'small tigers' (Godfrey, 1993). Low average labour costs open a window of opportunity for exports, capital inflows, and ultimately employment growth – but they clearly do not provide a guarantee. In both exports and FDI, other components of competitiveness are equally or even more important. A region-wide survey of FDI by Lankes and Venables (1996), for instance, concludes that the level of wages is not among the most important motivating factors for investors, but rather plays a role in locating the investment within the post-Soviet world. Investors for whom unskilled labour costs are an important factor tend to prefer CIS countries to CEE and the Baltics. Those attaching greater importance to skilled labour prefer the Czech Republic and Hungary to other countries, despite higher labour costs. Lankes and Venables argue that export-oriented investors put greater emphasis on local production costs, so at least a part of the potential FDI inflow may be significantly affected by wages in CEE relative to other potential host regions.

These caveats notwithstanding, low labour costs seem to be an important asset during the process of European integration. With technological renewal and improvements in other sources of competitiveness, low labour costs can *increasingly* contribute to the catch-up process of CEE countries. More exports and FDI can help create new jobs in the East but also generate concerns over displacement in the West – so-called social or wage dumping. Havlik (1996) argues that to eliminate the East–West wage disparities, CEE economies have to grow, and to grow they must export. Except for the complete abandonment of European integration, there is no alternative solution to this fundamental conflict of interests.

3.3.4   *Payroll and Other Taxes*

Depending on the relative elasticities of labour demand and supply, taxes can affect the evolution of labour costs both directly (payroll and income taxes) and indirectly via by introducing a wedge between the CPI and the PPI (value-added taxes). Payroll taxes are particularly high and undoubtedly enlarge the gap between take-home pay and labour costs. In 1995, the percentage tax rates on employers and employees, respectively, were 48 + 0 in Poland, 47 + 11 in Hungary, 35 + 12 in the Czech Republic and 38 + 12 in Slovakia (Coricelli et al., 1996, p. 43). Among EU countries, only Italy (46 + 10) and Belgium (34 + 13) had similarly high rates.

Though substantial tax cuts seem unlikely in the short run given the state of general and social security budgets, by expanding the tax base and cutting, for instance, unemployment-related taxes where the rate is declining, governments might try to reduce the payroll burden. Nevertheless, wage flexibility (the degree to which the tax burden will be shifted onto employees) seems a more relevant question than general tax cuts for the coming years. We would also argue that – as far as government action is concerned – a positive effect in the short run might be expected from the *restructuring* of the tax burden rather than from general tax cuts. Though the wages of low-paid workers fell considerably during the transition in all countries, the decline was insufficient to mitigate the decline in demand for their labour, and a policy of allowing an 'equilibrium level' of employment to emerge without accompanying social policy would appear politically difficult, if not impossible. Removing the payroll tax on low wages, for example, might have the desired effect for reducing the cost of low-skilled labour relative to skilled. We shall come back to this option in Chapter 4.

3.3.5   'Virtual' Charges

Employers who are forward-looking not only compare the productivity of additional workers with their observable labour costs, but also consider expected future wages as well as potential liabilities which may be implied by the employment relationship. Specifically, in the event that the worker's employment is not longer economically warranted, a dismissal may be costly. In Western Europe, for example, a redundancy is usually associated with a severance payment, but may also be linked to bureaucratic requirements, advance notification and other implicit costs. In conditions where large layoffs are necessary, a firm may need to formulate a 'social plan' with additional costs and other encumbrances. Thus, in addition to the usual amortization of training and hiring costs, it is natural that such regulations will drive an additional virtual wedge between observable labour costs and marginal productivity. As regards severance regulations, one might productively apply the reasoning of Dixit and Pindyck (1994), in which the hiring decision acquires an additional option value under certain conditions and embodies the ability to postpone that decision until more information is available. Should bad news arrive, the worker is not hired and the firm saves the severance costs. If a worker is hired, the employer exercises the option, and the value of that option is the value of waiting. In general, if the firm is in an 'average' state when the regulation is introduced, the demand for labour will be lower for any given wage level.[29]

Unfortunately, there is little empirical evidence on how redundancy payment obligations affect the firing and hiring decisions of CEE firms. A number of countries have introduced some form of severance regulations which are sometimes comparable to those found in the European Union, but the general opinion is that these regulations are not enforced in large segments of the economy. To the extent that this may change in the future, this topic will become relevant in Chapter 4 in the discussion of accession to the European Union.

3.4 Wage Flexibility

In the short to medium run, when the capital stock is fixed in size and quality, most of the burden of adjustment in a labour market which clears will fall on absolute and relative wage levels. Since wage structures still bear the marks of the state-socialist legacy, *wage flexibility* is a central issue. As this notion is rather fuzzy, it will be useful to distinguish between different aspects of wage flexibility, each important for the allocative functioning of the labour market.[30] First, wage flexibility means that relative wages adjust to shifts in demand, providing a correct orientation for both workers and employers. Second, wage flexibility requires the absence of administrative constraints, floors and caps, or other restrictions on wage setting. Third, it may also mean the lack of institutional arrangements resulting in leapfrogging, or other mechanisms implying a high-inflation, non-accelerating-inflation rate of unemployment (NAIRU).

Apart from the *level* of labour cost – which affects both export competitiveness and foreign direct investment (FDI) – the process of restructuring may also be fostered or stymied by relative wages. This will be especially true if labour is heterogeneous; workers will be hired according to their productivity in alternative uses, and relative wages in a clearing market will reflect relative scarcities as well as relative productivities. Relative scarcities will be determined by workers' decisions to be mobile, i.e. move from sectors with low wages to those with high wages. This will reflect the current wage differential as well as an assessment of future gains from the move, impatience, uncertainty, and the costs of mobility. Should the gap narrow relative to the market-determined benchmark, worker mobility will decline.

It follows that relative wages as an incentive to mobility have paramount importance in the transformation. This is especially true to the extent that the transformation occurs without unemployment, that is, as private firms expand while state enterprises contract. The less willing workers are to change firms on their own, the more likely it is that the state firms will be forced to lay off workers or even close. In the following sections, we examine not only the gap in mobility between new private firms and state enterprises, but also that between large and small firms, and between productivity and skill groups.

In the short run, flexibility in the relative wage structure will have little effect on relative supply; rather it will have the unpleasant side-effect of an increase in inequality. While this increase in inequality is politically and socially difficult to accept, it may provide the key mechanism for re-employing lower skilled young workers or older workers who were displaced from jobs in shrinking industries.

3.4.1   Evidence of Wage Flexibility – Regions

Attempts to capture the effect of unemployment on wages using regional data do not suggest a strong linkage between these two variables in CEE countries. Recent estimates by Boeri and Scarpetta (1996) for the Visegrad countries, for instance, resulted in correctly signed but insignificant parameters in equations relating regional wage change to the level and/or change of regional unemployment. Similarly, Commander and McHale (1995) report ambiguous results from these countries.

We would argue that the econometric estimates published so far are strongly affected by a too high level of aggregation which hides some of the spatial variation of unemployment rates and, more importantly, most of the variation of local wage rates.[31] The Hungarian case is instructive. Both Boeri and Scarpetta (1996) and Commander, Köllő and Ugaz (1994) estimate insignificant wage effects using unemployment statistics from 20 counties. In contrast, Kertesi and Köllő (1995, 1997) report robust effects using an exceptionally large sample of workers and distinguishing between 170 regions.[32] The elasticity of earnings with respect to the local unemployment rate increased substantially from −0.05 to −0.12. The 'wage curve' – a negative link between unemployment and wages – seems to have become more pronounced as open unemployment emerged. In 1994 and 1995 earnings are expected to decrease by 26–29% as we move from the lowest (5%) to the highest (35%) local unemployment rates, other things being equal. The effect of the short-term rate is stronger: comparing regions with 5% and 15% long-term unemployment, the wage difference is 7.1%. The difference between regions with 5% and 15% short-term unemployment is twice as large (14.6%). Demand shifts resulting in higher unemployment and lower wages simultaneously dominated the move along the demand curve. Holding the local unemployment rate in 1990 constant, larger wage cuts during the transition are associated with *higher* unemployment after the transition.

The findings on regional 'wage curves' in CEE are thus both scarce and contradictory. The results from Hungary may not hold for other countries, but indicate that sufficiently large and rich data sets may capture effects remaining unobserved at a higher level of aggregation. The wage elasticities estimated for this country fall to a range common in developed market economies. Though the Western results are themselves subject to considerable variation depending on specification and measurement levels, the elasticities seldom fall below −0.05 or exceed −0.2 (Winter-Ebmer, 1996). With values around −0.11 (and −0.15 for STU), the wage curve seems steeper in Hungary than in Germany, Norway or Austria, and quite similar to the United Kingdom.

At the same time that short-term wages appear responsive to local labour market conditions, the weaker wage pressure of long-term unemployment can potentially induce higher equilibrium unemployment and a sluggish reaction of employment to output *per se*. The former effect is obvious while the latter works through the rising share of long-term unemployment in an upswing. If the long-term unemployed search less intensively, or are less acceptable for firms, a rise in their share tends to reduce average search effectiveness, encourage wage claims, and reduce the rate of employment growth as discussed in Nickell (1995).[33]

3.4.2   Evidence from Skill Groups

Open unemployment hit all social groups in transforming CEE economies, but demand fell only slightly for college and university graduates, and even increased for skill and qualification levels. In all countries, wages and employment probabilities increase with education. Wages seem to have adjusted to the underlying relative demand shifts to a large extent. Earnings function estimates from five post-socialist countries (Table 3.6) suggest that the wages of workers with primary education fell by 2–4% *vis-à-vis* workers with vocational education and by 10% compared to secondary education. The wage gap between them and workers with higher education grew by rates between 12% and 30% depending on gender, period and country. Since these figures come from regressions not corrected for selectivity bias they yield lower-bound estimates of the change in offer wages.

Table 3.6   Percentage wage margins above the reference category in selected countries of transition (estimates from Mincer-type earnings functions)

	< Primary	Primary	Vocational	Secondary	College	University
Czech Republic						
1984[a]		ref.	8.3	21.0	36.8	
1992[a]		ref.	9.5	30.9	48.6	
Men[b]						
1988		ref.	5.0	13.5	34.4	
1992		ref.	9.3	23.4	46.0	
Women[b]						
1988		ref.	6.7	21.6	50.4	
1992		ref.	8.4	30.0	54.5	
Poland[d]						
1987			5.0 %/years in school			
1992			7.9 %/ years in school			
1993			7.3 %/ years in school			
Hungary[e]						
Men						
1986	−10.6	ref.	11.5	19.6	51.4	
1989	−4.2	ref.	12.1	27.2	70.4	
1992	−12.5	ref.	13.4	36.6	81.5	
Women						
1986	−18.3	ref.	14.4	25.4	63.9	
1989	−6.3	ref.	15.3	32.3	77.8	
1992	−12.5	ref.	17.4	37.5	80.3	
Slovakia[a]						
1984		ref.	8.3	21.0	36.8	
1992		ref.	11.0	30.9	50.7	
Slovenia[c]						
Men						
1987	ref.	4.4	16.3	31.9	52.0	71.5
1991	ref.	10.7	20.1	40.6	67.7	94.3
Women						
1987	ref.	7.9	16.4	37.0	56.9	76.8
1991	ref.	11.2	18.3	46.5	68.5	94.0

Source: estimated variable, explanatory variables.
[a] Sakova (1996), gross earnings, gender, experience, experience^2, schooling dummies.
[b] Vecernik (1995), gross earnings, experience, experience^2, schooling dummies.
[c] Orazem and Vodopivec (1995), hourly earnings, gender, experience, experience^2, schooling dummies, ethnicity, region, industry.
[d] Rutkowski (1996a), net earnings, gender, experience, experience^2, years in school, industry.
[e] Kertesi and Köllő (1997), gross earnings, experience, experience^2, schooling dummies.

While the return to general education increased unambiguously during the transition, the return to general labour market experience acquired under socialism did not. Demand for new types of experience-based skills implied flatter age–productivity profiles. The implication is similar if there is an increased need for firm-specific human capital investment, the horizon of which is shorter, and hence the cost greater, in the case of elderly workers. Two outcomes are possible: either wages fall for older workers, or job availability for them is reduced. Since dismissing older workers incurs specific costs or violates procedural rules (seniority-based severance payments, first-in last-out practices) the hiring side provides a solid justification for studying age-specific labour market positions. Most – albeit not all – studies report lower job-finding probability with elderly unemployed workers. Clear supporting evidence has been presented for Slovenia and Hungary.[34] The Polish results are similar but weaker. Contradictory evidence comes primarily from the Czech Republic and Slovakia.

How wages were affected is shown by an overview of earnings–experience profiles before and during the transition in Figure 3.2. While wages of the elderly grew in Slovenia (1987–91), returns to experience fell slightly in Hungary (1989–92 and 1994), more so in Poland (1987–92), while the magnitude of change was largest in the Czech and Slovak Republics (1984–92, 1987–92).[35] For illustrating the size of the estimated change, we might consider two workers with five and 25 years past work experience respectively, in Hungary. The earnings differential explained by this difference was 31.4 percentage points in 1989. Five years later, the elderly worker had 30 years of experience, and the younger one had 10,

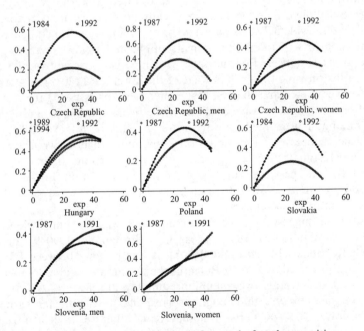

Figure 3.2 Experience-earnings profiles before and after the transition. Estimates from Mincer-type earnings functions

provided they both worked throughout the transition period. The associated differential between them declined to 25.4% by 1994, causing an additional 5.9% relative wage loss for the elderly worker. Similar calculations suggest a relative wage loss of 12.4% in Poland (1987–92), 19.6% for Czech women, and 32.2% for Czech men (1987–92). These latter figures may seem exaggerated but they are in line with Sakova's (1996) estimate of 25.3% for both sexes in 1984–92. Wages increased little or not at all for the elderly in Slovenia and Hungary but a price is paid for that in terms of job-finding probabilities steeply decreasing with age. In the Czech and Slovak cases, a substantial wage loss is observed and job-finding probabilities are roughly equal in all age groups. (Poland appears to lie between the extremes.) At this point, the data suggest substantial cross-country differences in the degree to which demand shifts have been accommodated by wages.[36]

3.4.3   Constraints: Minimum Wages and TIP

At the start of transition most CEE countries abolished the 'wage tariff' systems imposed on enterprises and introduced a statutory minimum wage. Since then there has been practically no other legal restriction on wage *levels*. Table 3.7 gives an overview of minimum wages compared to some moments of the earnings distribution, and follows changes over time in six countries. For the sake of comparison, we use the P5 and P10 ratios showing the median wage of the lower 10% (20%) of workers to the overall median. The first best comparison for assessing the relative level of the minimum wage could be made by comparing P5 and P10 to the minimum wage/median wage ratio. As this is not available from published sources, we use the ratio of minimum wage to average wage; this underestimates the relevant ratio by 5–10 percentage points depending on the skewness and kurtosis of the wage distribution. For Hungary we add a column showing the minimum wage/median wage ratio along with P5 and P10 earnings.

The data suggest that the minimum wage was certainly below the median of the lowest 10% of earnings throughout 1990–93 in the Czech Republic, Hungary and Poland; it was roughly between P5 and P10 earnings in Slovakia. In Bulgaria the minimum wage amounted to 52.7% of the average wage (and presumably at least 55–60% of the median wage) in 1991 that roughly corresponds to the median earnings of the lower 20% of workers in that year. Likewise, in Romania the statutory minimum wage/median wage ratio may have been higher than the P10 ratio. At least in the latter two countries, the minimum

Table 3.7 Minimum wage and earnings at the bottom of the wage distribution

Country	P5	P10	Minimum wage/ average wage	Minimum wage/ median
Bulgaria				
1990	55.9	63.3	44.6	–
1991	46.8	56.3	52.7	–
1992	–	–	35.9	–
1993	50.8	56.9	38.3	–
Czech Republic				
1991	55.2	62.9	51.1	–
1992	54.4	60.7	45.9	–
1993	51.4	57.0	36.5	–
Hungary				
1990	51.0	57.7	42.0	–
1991	–	–	39.1	–
1992	49.1	56.6	36.0	43.3
1993	47.2	55.9	33.0	41.1
Poland				
1990	–	–	21.4	–
1991	53.6	61.6	34.9	–
1992	53.8	61.6	37.5	–
1993	52.4	60.1	41.0	–
Romania				
1990	–	–	73.0	–
1991	58.1	66.8	62.6	–
1992	–	–	59.0	–
1993	51.9	61.1	37.2	–
Slovakia				
1989	54.7	62.9	–	
1991	–	–	52.0	
1993	61.6	64.9	42.1	

P5: median of bottom 10% to overall median.
P10: median of bottom 20% to overall median.
Source: Rutkowski (1996a) for P5 and P10. EC8 (1995) for minimum/average wage. Kertesi and Köllő (1997) for minimum/median wage in Hungary.
Underlined: figures above and below are not strictly comparable.

wage was set at relatively high levels and/or Romanian and Bulgarian firms did not respect the mandatory floor.

Statutory minimum wages have been decreasing in relative terms since their introduction everywhere except Poland, and by 1993 they were far below earnings of the worst-paid 10% of the labour force. (This holds for Poland as well.) The P5 and P10 ratios have themselves been decreasing in four out of six countries, so it is not likely that the minimum wage pushed up actual earnings at the lower tail of the distribution and became relatively 'low' for that reason. In Bulgaria and Romania, the P5 ratios increased, so in their case one cannot rule out the possibility that minimum wages put an upward pressure on low wages. The minimum wage/ average wages ratios, however, dropped from 52% to 38% in Bulgaria and 62% to 37% in Romania by 1993 and were already well below the P5 ratio in that year.

Very little is known about the employment effect of the minimum wage. Given its proximity to what was actually paid to many workers in 1990–91, at least in Bulgaria and Romania, one can not *a priori* exclude such an effect. The authors in the comprehensive volume on CEE minimum wages edited by Standing and Vaughan-Whitehead (1995) argue against this presumption. Among the authors of the book, however, only Buchtiková (1995) makes an attempt to quantify the possible implications by calculating how the wage bill would be affected by a rise in the minimum wage and whether sales revenues could accommodate the given change. She detects a minor impact (1% employment loss for the doubling of the minimum wage) but her calculation seems to ignore an indirect effect that works through induced wage increase in groups earning slightly more than the minimum.

The minimum wage/average wage ratios are now in a range of 33–41%, well below similar ratios in OECD countries with minimum wage legislation. It therefore seems unlikely that minimum wages now have any significant impact on labour demand. At the same time, benefits are tied to the minimum wage in some countries, so a substantial increase could affect labour demand through fiscal channels but such a rise seems rather unlikely at the present.

We now turn to restrictions on wage setting 'from above' or taxes on excessive wage growth – sometimes called TIPs (tax-based incomes policies). It is important to note that, apart from Russia and Hungary, most CEE countries restricted tax-based incomes policies to state firms. Poland and the Czech Republic removed the TIP but reintroduced it later (this actually happened for the second time in 1997 in the latter country). The main argument for a TIP is that a high tax rate can reduce the equilibrium rate of unemployment by reducing 'leap-frogging' (the race between firms to keep up with inflation and each other in wage setting). The arguments against a TIP are that it distorts relative wages, it punishes fast productivity-cum-wage growth, and it is difficult to administer.

The ambivalence of the Polish and Czech governments to a TIP indicates the great uncertainty concerning the benefits and costs of these policies. It is hard to assess how much leap-frogging is currently occurring in CEE economies. As far as the counter-arguments are concerned, these also seem to be based on general considerations and convictions rather than established stylized facts drawn after circumspect investigation, although the experience of the industrialized world with TIPs in the 1970s was almost uniformly negative.

3.5   Sectoral Differences – The Risk of a 'Spillover Effect'

CEE labour markets can hardly be regarded as homogeneous entities with uniform rules of wage setting and labour regulations. Some firms engage in collective bargaining with well-organized unions; are subject to tough fiscal supervision, excess wage taxes, severance regulations, redundancy payment obligations or working time restrictions; other firms are exempt from these rules or successfully evade them. Though the differences between firms are more of degree than type, it is not misleading to speak of a 'regulated' versus an 'unregulated' sector in these economies. In the regulated sector we likely find more state-owned and large firms; monopoly positions are more frequent; labour is better organized. In the unregulated sector, where most new jobs were created, firms are small and privately owned. Under such conditions there is a risk that high wages (or regulations implying high non-wage costs) hinder job creation in the emerging, unregulated segments of the economy. The risk of such a spillover effect is high if: (i) the emerging sectors have to adjust take-home pay to levels prevailing in the contracting sectors; (ii) wage restraints are weaker in the contracting sectors; and (iii) regulations in question are enforced in the private or small-firm sectors. The following sections discuss the relevance of these points.

3.5.1   *Sectoral Wage Differentials*

In order to attract workers, maintain adequate incentives and control labour turnover, emerging firms are likely to pay at least the same wage, in terms of take-home pay, as do former state enterprises. In principle, until the demand for external labour in the state sector was low, they could set lower wages but we find no evidence that this option was frequently chosen. In countries where data are available, private and foreign firms seem to pay equal or higher wages than state enterprises. The picture is admittedly less clear when we compare large and small firms.

The private-state wage gap. The data on differentials between private and state sector wages seem to be highly sensitive to the inclusion/exclusion of small establishments and self-employment. The survey-based observations typically include these categories and indicate higher earnings in the private sector. For Poland, Rutkowski (1996b) shows an 11% margin above state sector wages on average using labour force survey data. The differentials range from 3% for workers with vocational training to 27% for university graduates. In the Czech Republic, Vecernik (1995) observed that earnings in privatized firms were 10% higher than in state enterprises, 20% higher in new private firms, and 70–75% higher in self-employment in 1993 and 1994. Like Vecernik, Flanagan (1995b) used data from the 1993 wave of the Survey of Economic Attitudes and Expectations and estimated a 30% margin above state sector wages using a state/private dummy in a Mincerian earnings function. Similar estimates in Hungary by Commander et al. (1994) using household panel survey data suggested a 5–10% margin above state sector earnings in 1992 depending on the definition of earnings and sectors. In Hungary, wage gains from entering the private rather than the state sector after a spell of unemployment, as reported by workers themselves, were in a range of 4–8% for job losers and 10–15% for job leavers. Job leavers starting their own business reported a 52% gain over entrants to the state sector, while job losers after a short spell anticipated a 24% gain and those after a long spell a 9% gain.[37]

The establishment-based data generally exclude the smallest firms and – where available – indicate lower wages in the private sector as long as raw data are compared. Official statistics suggest that wages were *lower* in domestic private firms by 1.8% in the Czech Republic and 13.5% in Slovakia in 1992 as reported in Benácek (1995). Kertesi and Köllö (1997) found that average earnings in domestic private firms with 20 or more workers were lower by 10–15% in 1992–5 compared to majority state-owned firms in Hungary. Controlling for other wage determinants, however, reduces the observed wage gap substantially. Controlling for demographic and human capital variables reduces the raw gap between state and private firms from 9.6% to 7.7%; controlling for industry reduces it to 3%. Taking firm size, location, productivity and the capital–labour ratio into account brought down the estimated ownership-specific difference to zero. In all years the pure difference remained below 2%. Combining these results and adding what we know from newspapers, anecdotes and personal experience, one could conclude that earnings in the private sector are presumably higher but the differences diminish as we move from self-employment and small firms to medium-sized and large enterprises.[38]

Foreign firms. There is clear evidence that foreign firms on average pay more than state enterprises or domestic private firms. The establishment-based figures hint at a margin above state firms of 8.9% in Slovakia (1992), 17.5% in Czech Republic (1992) and 30% in Hungary (1992, 1995).[39] Despite a gap in terms of raw figures, we cannot take for granted that foreign firms pay so much above the going market price of the type of workers they actually employ. Holding gender, age and education constant, the advantage in Hungary (1995) comes down from 30% to

18%. Allowing for differences in industrial composition modifies the estimate to 21%. Holding the firm's average product constant reduces the difference to 9%, suggesting that the wage advantage of foreign firms partly rests on their higher productivity. Basu et al. (1994) present similar results for the Czech Republic (1992–3) in that they find the advantage of foreign firms to be smaller once productivity is controlled for. Furthermore, a part of both the productivity gap and the wage gap may stem from unobserved differences in human capital endowments. Standard econometric earnings functions linking wages to observable skills tend to *underestimate* the earnings of workers in foreign firms in Hungary, especially in the case of skilled workers and university graduates. These workers may be, at least partly, paid more because the firm has to reward their better quality (language skills, for instance) and resulting higher productivity. In Hungary, where foreign firms are particularly numerous, it is easy to observe that they generally screen workers carefully and provide more training than do domestic firms. Filer et al. (1995) present similar observations from the Czech Republic: hiring and training costs amounted to 9.3% of the earnings bill of foreign-owned firms compared to 3.1% in state firms, 2.9% in domestic private firms and 3.4% in (mostly small) joint ventures, in 1992. Screening and training leads to better quality and higher wages holding observables constant. On the other hand, hiring and training costs increase wages *per se*, since the losses implied by labour turnover are higher so a higher take-home pay may actually reduce total labour costs.

The firm-size wage gap. Results from both the Czech Republic and from Hungary suggest a marked increase in the relative wages paid by larger firms.[40] The wage margin in favour of large enterprises was small before the transition in both countries. In Czechoslovak manufacturing, the single largest firm of an industry had an advantage of 4.6% over the industry mean, on average, and the largest four firms had an advantage of 2% in 1989. These differences roughly tripled by 1992 rising to 12.3% and 7.3%, respectively. In Hungary, the gap between the largest firms (over 3000 employees) and firms with 20–50 workers was 1% in 1989 but 23.9% 1995. The difference between the size categories 1000–3000 and 50–300 grew from 1.5 to 12% after controlling for other variables.

Two important caveats apply when we evaluate these figures. First, the growing underreporting of wages in small firms may partly explain the widening firm-size wage gap. Second, one might note that under socialism the wage gap between large 'priority firms' and the rest of the economy was relatively small. In fact, large firms typically suffered from particularly grave labour shortages and could hardly have maintained adequate manning levels without direct support from the authorities. Support was given in various forms ranging from higher enrolment quotas in vocational training to administrative measures constraining hiring in non-priority areas. The deficit of labour turnover (excess of quits over hires from the market) was offset by an influx of school leavers, by forced mergers, or even direct allocation. At the moment these barriers and non-market practices were abolished the *existing* wage differential was insufficient for equalizing non-pecuniary disadvantages such as multiple shifts, inflexible worktime, environmental hazards and other attributes of large industrial organizations. At the same time, it means that the inherited wage gap could easily ensure a net voluntary flow from large firms to smaller enterprises.

3.5.2   Predatory Wage Setting?

If large state-owned firms set wages high relative to productivity – and the emerging private firms have to keep up with them in terms of take-home pay as suggested by the data – job creation could be adversely affected. Alternatively, emerging firms will be tempted to reduce labour cost by the evasion of taxes and other regulations. A recent multi-country survey of enterprises in seven CEE countries by Pohl et al. (1997) lends support to these concerns. In most countries, real wages in state-owned firms grew faster than productivity; in all countries but Poland, real wages increased at least as fast in privatized firms as in state firms. At the same time, private firms tended to keep wage growth within the limits of their own productivity growth.

These and similar results call for creating stronger wage restraints in some parts of the economy by excess wage tax applied in a selective fashion. Beyond doubt, the risk of 'excessive' wage growth is higher in the state sector or among larger enterprises in general. Imposing a TIP in the state sector or in the large-firm sector is likely to lead to both Type I and Type II errors. This is nicely illustrated by Figure 3.3, where Hungarian state firms and private firms are compared in terms of productivity growth and real wage growth in 1993. The disparity observed in the survey of Pohl et al. (1997) at least partly holds: state firms increased the real product wage by 4.6%, while real value added/worker increased by 7.6%. In private firms wages grew by 0.5% and productivity increased by 11% on average. The dispersion within the two groups was substantial, however: roughly half of the firms had wage growth above productivity growth in each group. These data suggest that the state–private distinction is too blunt for detecting the source of 'excessive' wage growth.

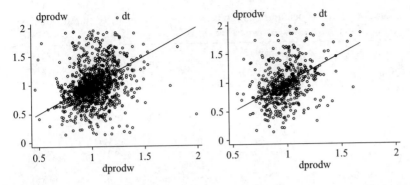

Figure 3.3 Real value added/worker and real product wage in Hungarian
state (left) and private (right) firms (1993/1992, log scales).
Source: National Labour Centre Wage Survey, firms interviewed in both 1992
and 1993. Number of observations: 1273 state firms, 577 private firms.
Ownership defined on the basis of majority share. Fitted values b[exp]exp +
b[exp^2]exp^2 plotted with exp. The sources for b[exp] and b[exp^2]: Czech
Republic and Slovakia 1984 and 1992: Sakova (1996), Table 6; Czech
Republic 1987 and 1992, by gender: Vecernik (1996), 361; Hungary 1989,
1992 and 1994: Kertesi and Köllő (1997); Poland 1987 and 1992: Rutkowski
(1996b), Table 6, columns 1 and 3; Slovenia 1987 and 1991, by gender:
Vodopivec (1995), Table 7

Similarly, after substantial changes in the behaviour of many large
state enterprises, it does not necessarily follow that state sector workers – as a group – are in a much better bargaining position. Clearly, the
risk that state sector workers cause damage to private sector employment
is higher if the elasticity of labour demand with respect to wages is high in
the private sector but low in the state sector. Unfortunately, the available
studies fail to discuss this important issue. For the sake of illustration,
Table 3.8 presents labour demand equations from Hungary estimated
separately for state and domestic private firms using 1993 data. Impact
multipliers suggest larger short-term employment response to wage
change in private firms, but long-term effects are similar. Using the parameters of the contemporaneous and lagged wage and employment terms,
we can estimate that a 20% rise in wages reduces employment by 9.2% in
the state sector, 10.8% in the domestic private sector, 11.5% in mixed
and 12.3% in foreign firms over a two-year period following the shock.
The results are similar in Table 3.9, in which small and larger firms are
compared. Here again we find that the distinction between 'state and
private' or 'large and small' are inadequate for capturing current differences in bargaining positions.[41]

These findings – illustrative as they are – call attention to the idea that
governments should identify the locus of predatory wage setting carefully

Table 3.8   Labour demand equations estimated for majority state-owned, private, foreign and mixed-ownership firms

	State	Private	Foreign	Mixed
E_{t-1}	0.7714	0.7473	0.7123	0.8562
	(33.9)	(29.6)	(15.5)	(30.9)
Q	0.2718	0.3163	0.1844	0.3107
	(9.8)	(10.7)	(2.7)	(8.9)
Q_{t-1}	−0.0595	−0.0929	0.0547	−0.1733
	(−2.5)	(−2.9)	(0.6)	(−4.5)
W	−0.4444	−0.5474	−0.5374	−0.5868
	(−4.7)	(−7.1)	(−3.1)	(−8.1)
W_{t-1}	0.2598	0.3306	0.1983	0.4298
	(2.9)	(4.3)	(1.3)	(5.8)
Constant	2.0578	2.4619	3.8481	1.6812
	(5.8)	(6.7)	(5.2)	(3.4)
adj. R^2	0.9642	0.9384	0.9789	0.9672
Root MSE	0.2196	0.2158	0.1794	0.1854
No. of observations	1207	561	128	428

*Mixed stands for firms with majority owner's share below 50% and firms with unknown ownership. Firms are randomly selected. An introduction to the sample is given in Köllő; (1996).
Hungary, National Labour Centre Wage Survey data, 1993
Linear regressions with Huber standard errors
Dependent: employment (E). Explanatory: W = average wage, Q = value added, All variables in logs, 7 industry dummies added.

Table 3.9   Labour demand equations estimated for small and large firms

	Large $E_{t-1} > 100$	Small $E_{t-1} \leq 100$	*F*-tests for the equality of parameters
E_{t-1}	0.7843	0.7619	1.18
	(51.2)	(37.1)	(0.278)
Q	0.3051	0.2476	17.9
	(25.3)	(18.3)	(0.000)
Q_{t-1}	−0.0952	−0.0377	10.23
	(−6.3)	(−2.1)	(0.001)
W	−0.5189	−0.4697	1.29
	(−12.4)	(−10.8)	(0.255)
W_{t-1}	0.2891	0.2621	0.36
	(6.6)	(5.8)	(0.551)
		Joint :	0.85
		(W, W_{t-1})	(0.427)
Constant	2.4563	2.329	
	(8.9)	(8.7)	
Average wage	31,826	30,920	
adj. R^2	0.9472	0.8067	
Root MSE	0.2142	0.2079	
No. of observations	1393	940	

Sample and notation as with Table 3.9.

before considering incomes policies. Discriminatory policies against the state sector and/or large firms in general – appearing in the TIP practices of several countries – can also lead to price distortions in the labour market. Though the risk of a spillover effect exists (leading from 'predatory wage setting' in some firms to less job creation in others), there remains a lack of reliable information for the appropriate design of wage policies. If the exact source of distortion cannot be justified by such economic evidence in a particular country and period, these policies should be avoided.

3.5.3   *Extending and Enforcing Regulations*

Though it is difficult to demonstrate, it is evident that a number of regulations are evaded in the private and/or small-enterprise sectors of CEE economies. Informal, unregistered employment is widespread, redundancy rules or worktime restrictions are not observed, taxes are not fully paid. The attitude of the governments towards this phenomenon is admittedly ambiguous, since a tough enforcement of the regulations would predictably imply non-trivial loss of output and employment. Deeper integration with the EU will inevitably raise this issue. Western competitors and unions may complain about 'unfair competition' on the part of Eastern producers effectively exempt from European regulations. Likewise, cooperation between Western and Eastern trade unions may increase the pressure for the enforcement of rules. It is possible that EU accession could have an adverse impact on labour demand through this channel, and this issue is taken up in detail in Chapter 4.

3.6   Conclusions

The evidence reviewed in this chapter calls attention to several problems which could limit employment growth during the post-transformation recovery. First, it appears unlikely that the rate of growth of self-employment and small and medium-sized enterprises will persist in the future, since the scope for further 'gap-filling investment' is limited compared with the early stages of transition. Convergence to industrial structures in market economy patterns has progressed to a point at which output and employment patterns resemble those in countries of similar economic development. Second, several factors reducing the demand for outside labour and raising the cost of job creation were identified. Overstaffing in large state enterprises is hardly a negligible problem in countries where enterprise restructuring was slow. The deficiencies of the inherited capital stock will imply that employment growth is heavily dependent on physical capital formation. Despite dramatic real wage declines, labour costs have failed to fall in several countries. While some of the causes raising labour costs (changes in turnover taxation, elimination of subsidies, etc.) have disappeared, others – like high rates of payroll taxation – persist, while future burdens associated with the enforcement of labour market regulations may increase as well. The issue of wage restraint will therefore become an increasingly relevant issue.

The empirical findings on wage flexibility give a far from clear picture. The influence of unemployment on pay appears to vary substantially across countries, while statistical results seem sensitive to measurement levels and estimation techniques. We do find evidence that private and privatized firms are more successful in keeping wage growth below productivity growth. At the same time, it is difficult to identify the source of 'predatory wage setting' to the extent it exists, along the categories of firm ownership or size. Returning to socialist-type wage control, even if restricted to state enterprises, raises the usual risks and problems associated with income policies.

Besides building a functional system of collective bargaining – with special emphasis on agreements keeping wages growth below that of productivity, enforcement of the negotiated outcomes, competition between unions, and representation of the unemployed – governments could help the recovery of employment in several ways. An important field of action seems to lie in the small enterprise sectors in which sole proprietorships (as opposed to small capitalist enterprises) are still heavily over-represented. Under the special conditions of the post-socialist transition employment could largely benefit from a regulatory framework which encourages physical capital formation in general, and foreign direct investment in particular. Last but not least, governments should elaborate a long-term strategy of reducing the heavy tax burden on wages.

Notes

1. See Góra et al. (1996) and Earle and Oprescu (1995), respectively.
2. This is true for Poland, 1989 compared to 1990, and Hungary, 1990 compared to 1991. For 1989 they estimate the employment/output elasticity to be 2.67 in a sample of 100 Hungarian firms – a value of about 5–10 times the levels found elsewhere. This deviation reflects, among other things, measurement error.
3. For evidence in Hungary, see Köllő: (1997).
4. See Basu et al. (1994) for a Czechoslovak–Polish comparison or Estrin and Svejnar (1996) for estimates on Czech, Polish and Hungarian firms.
5. For labour costs see Blanchard et al. (1995), pp. 307–309. The benefit/average wage ratio was highest among CEE countries until 1991; compare EC8 (1995), p. 42.

6. See Burda (1994), Aghion and Blanchard (1994), and Castanheira and Roland (1996).
7. Blanchard et al. (1995), p. 319. The official inflow rate (0.5) for Hungary was later revised to 1% per month by Micklewright and Nagy (1994), who detected a major underestimation for technical reasons.
8. Self-employment grew from 243 000 in 1983 to 501 000 in 1990 in Hungary. Similarly, non-agricultural self-employment grew by 34% already in 1986–91 in Slovenia (Drobnic and Rus 1993).
9. EC8 (1995), p. 36 except Slovenia where the figure relates to 1986 and comes from Drobnic and Rus (1993).
10. $(\Delta S/ - \Delta P = 0.27$ and $\Delta U/ - \Delta P = 0.59$ as opposed to the actual 0.52 and 0.20, respectively).
11. A fourth, technical conclusion is that labour turnover figures are evidently downwards-biased by the exclusion of flows into self-employment.
12. Formally, $pos_t = \Sigma_{exp}(n_{t,i} - n_{t-1,i})/\Sigma(n_t + n_{t-1})/2$ where *exp* relates to the set of expanding sectors. Similarly, *neg* is defined as $neg_t = -\Sigma_{contr}(n_{t,i} - n_{t-1,i})/\Sigma(n_t + n_{t-1})$ /2 where *contr* stands for contracting units.
13. The periods observed are split into a first and a second state separated by the change of the industrial code system, so the estimates cover different periods country by country, and the data usually do not comprise the twelve months between mid-1992 and mid-1993. While a shortcoming, there is no better solution if we want to measure the intensity of structural change rather than the extent of the statistical reform. In addition to the industrial data, for Poland and Hungary expanding and contracting *enterprises* are also compared using results from Konings et al. (1996) and this project.
14. The hypothesis assumes linkage between per capita income and sectoral composition or sectoral growth.
15. Note that the Hungarian figures cover only 1989–91.
16. This happens to be true for advanced industrial countries as well; see Davis and Haltiwanger (1993).
17. The point is not that spin-offs should be generally treated as a statistical artifact with no economic meaning; since intra-enterprise transactions were strongly preferred to market transactions under socialism (with the aim to simplify control and coping with input shortages) the break-up of large units could increase overall productivity by reducing transaction costs. Almost all the new jobs were created by new firms during the transition, but some of the new firms were actually spin-offs of old firms.
18. For examples of this region-wide practice in the Czech Republic, see Benácek (1995).
19. *The OECD Observer*, 1994.
20. Note that these figures relate to different time periods so caution is warranted when making cross-country comparisons.
21. Johnson's (1994) survey goes further by claiming 'there are no remaining barriers to private sector growth that can be rapidly removed by government action' (in Poland, Hungary and the Czech Republic) (p. 256).
22. In Poland and Romania the ratios are much lower but, considering that many service-related enterprises are counted as agriculture and excluded from the comparative statistics cited here, they are probably underestimated.
23. Though open and hidden subsidies still exist, especially in the form of tax arrears (Schaffer 1995), they mostly help retain jobs in unprofitable large firms and seem to have only indirect effect on the cost of job creation.
24. See Sargent (1978), Nickell (1986).
25. See for example the discussion in Snower (1995), pp. 121–123.
26. Furthermore, we cannot rule out the possibility of a substitution effect as firms adopt technologies developed in high-wage Western economies.
27. See Bean (1989), Burda (1988a) and Blanchard et al. (1986).
28. It is worth emphasizing that in the case of the latter countries the price and wage indices may be misleading because of well-known problems: particularly grave shortages in the base period, sharp changes in the composition of consumption bundles, and the appearance of new goods unavailable in the old regime.

29. Naturally, if the firm is in a high employment state when the regulation is introduced, it will tend to increase labour demand; this is one reason for the ambiguity often cited in the literature. These conditions can hardly be expected to apply to Central and Eastern Europe, however.
30. For a discussion see Bruno and Sachs (1985) or Layard et al. (1991).
31. In Hungary, distinguishing between the 20 regions and the 170 labour office areas suggests, for instance, that only 49% of the variance of unemployment and 19% of the variance of average wages were accounted for by between-region differences.
32. The survey covers about 150 000 randomly selected workers in 1986, 1989 and 1992–5. The individual earnings regression functions estimated for these samples are controlled for gender, age, education, industry, and firm characteristics including size, productivity and the capital–labour ratio. To allow for a wage curve present already before the transition the unemployment rates of 1992 were used in the equations for 1986 and 1989. From 1993 onwards, a distinction was made between the short-term and the long-term unemployment rates.
33. The assumption that the weakness of the wage pressure has to do with the 'employ-ability' of the long-term unemployed is supported by Boeri's (1994b) panel estimates of a matching function of the form: $O = f$ (STU, LTU, V). The effect on job finding of STU proved markedly stronger than the effect of LTU in the four Visegrad countries, and in Slovakia and Hungary the elasticities of O with respect to LTU were not sig-nificantly different from zero.
34. Drobnic and Rus (1993), Vodopivec (1995), Micklewright and Nagy (1994), Köllő and Nagy (1995). Steiner and Kwiatkowski (1995) found low exit rates for job-seekers aged 45 and above. Puhani's (1996) estimates indicate a job hazard rate falling with age, too, though some of the presented coefficients are not significant at conventional levels. Similarly, Dorenboos (1996) found the reemployment rate falling with age in both Hungary and Poland but the results for the latter country were not significant. Ham, Svejnar and Terrell (1995) found the exit rate falling as workers pass age 40 in the CR, but no age effect in Slovakia. Terrell, Lubyová and Strapec (1995) observed no age effect in Slovak districts, and *positive* in the Czech regions. Lubyová and van Ours (1996) also conclude that age has no marked effect on exit probability in Slovakia.
35. One should also notice that the returns to experience in CEE, post-transition, are low in absolute terms. Comparing East and West Germany, Steiner and Bellmann (1995) conclude that 'experience-earnings profiles are very flat (and) it will take a long time before we observed profiles as steep as for West Germany' (p. 557). The intra-German comparison seems particularly interesting as a series of important factors (like union pay scales or state regulations) are automatically controlled for. It might be added that the profile they present for men (coefficients of 0.0411 for age and −0.0150 for age squared in a selectivity-bias corrected earnings function) is steeper than any of those cited in Figure 3.3 of this chapter.
36. We mention here that in both Slovenia and Hungary *reemployment wages* do fall with experience (Orazem *et al.*, 1995; Köllő and Nagy, 1996). The bias towards employment rather than wage adjustment is nevertheless apparent from the earnings functions esti-mates on the sample of all workers.
37. See Köllő and Nagy (1996).
38. This is partly so because self-employed workers, or those involved in very small firms, are on average more qualified and the returns to education and experience are generally higher in the private sector (Rutkowski, 1996b; Flanagan, 1995b) but it also seems to hold if these differences are held constant.
39. See Benácek (1995) and Kertesi and Köllő (1997).
40. See Zemplinerová and Stíbel (1996), and Kertesi and Köllő (1997). We lack information on firm size effects from countries other than the Czech Republic and Hungary but assume that their case is not exceptional.
41. The same seems to hold for splitting the economy into unionized and non-unionized sectors. The limited evidence available is rather discouraging. Basu et al. (1994) found no significant union effect on employment or wages in Polish enterprise samples. In the Czech Republic, Flanagan (1995b) estimated negative or zero coefficients for a

unionized workplace in individual earnings functions, depending on controls. While there is evidence of union militancy in highly monopolized or favoured industries like mining in Romania, power and gas in Hungary, or the state railways in almost all countries, available statistical results do not support a strong overall union effect on wages.

4
The Role of Policy

As a guiding principle, policy interventions in labour markets should be justified by failures or distortions, and should be linked in the first instance to *efficiency* and not equity concerns.[1] Yet distortions underlying government intervention in labour markets are rarely if ever explicitly discussed. It is not difficult to find them in industrial economies: labour unions, employers' associations, monopsonies, or efficiency wages; governments themselves may also distort incentives via taxation, unemployment benefits, minimum wages, and severance laws. Labour supply may be affected by income taxation and the social safety net, early retirement policies and the minimum working age. Many interventions can in fact be justified on efficiency as well as redistributive and political economic grounds; for example, unemployment benefits protect certain types of human capital investments from overly hasty depreciation or abandonment, but also do so in an actuarially unfair (and redistributive) way. In the context of systemic transformation, additional distortions arise from asymmetric information, absence of well-understood or well-defined property rights, incomplete information about workers' qualifications and skills, lack of coordination in decision-making, poorly organized labour markets with potential for search externalities, and high mobility costs arising from malfunctioning housing and property markets.

This chapter studies the role of policy for labour markets in the Central and East European economies. Its emphasis and recommendations are motivated by issues identified in Chapters 2 and 3, as well as the general need to discuss the role of the government in these economies. While it is important to refute a blind presumption for paring back the government, it is also important to prevent or retard the formation of labour market institutions often associated with inflexibility in Western Europe. In the end, each institution and policy should be judged on a case-by-case basis, but also in the context of its interactions with other institutions and policies.

In contrast to Chapters 2 and 3, the ideas set out in the following pages are tentative and largely speculative, as they require an assessment of relevant policies as well as their effects. Three central themes are discussed. First, we stress the fine balancing act required of social policies between cushioning the blow of transition and inhibiting its progress. Restrictive administration of unemployment benefits, for example, will accelerate the restructuring of the labour force but will also increase the costs on the social welfare system. Fiscal traps can be the consequence if labour is taxed to shoulder the burden. Well-designed active labour markets policies are one potential means of avoiding this trade-off. Another is trying to integrate the informal economy – which may represent up to half of GDP in some countries – into the taxed formal sector. This may require fundamental reforms of the tax system.

A second theme is the accession to the European Union, which remains a central policy objective of all CEE economies. Because of its indirect implications for labour market policy, accession to the European Union involves risks as well as rewards. Structural change, which in the first instance is felt by labour markets, will be difficult to achieve even without the EU. Labour market experiences of EU accessions over the past 25 years have not been uniformly negative, nor have they been uniformly positive, as our empirical results show. We identify some of the risks associated with EU accession for CEE labour markets and labour market policy.

Finally, education and human capital policy is a logical use of resources for preparing the CEE labour force for challenges of the coming decades. Generous early retirement provisions in CEE induced massive scrapping of human capital; while young people have a better chance of getting a job, the evidence suggests that the general human capital stock in terms of basic secondary education is inadequate compared with OECD countries. Now that retirement ages may be raised, education policy will make even more claims on public resources for retooling both young and old people. Given the relatively poor secondary educational record of the CEE countries (despite a widespread view to the contrary) it would seem that increased spending on education – as opposed to training – is a more appropriate use of resources.

4.1 Income Support for the Unemployed

4.1.1 Potential Efficiency Costs of Passive Unemployment Support in the Transition

The vision of Europe to which the CEE economies are striving to return can be described as a market economy with a concern for avoiding excessive income inequality and a tradition of state-managed solidarity with the less fortunate. It was only natural that strains placed on individuals during the course of the transformation would give rise to political demands for social insurance. Unemployment benefit systems were introduced at the outset of the transition process as a response to this need; in addition, they relieved employers of many social responsibilities and allowed them to focus on enterprise restructuring. In most CEE countries, programmes of unemployment compensation, early retirement, social assistance, and severance pay were implemented soon after governments had committed themselves to market transformation, but well before their financial consequences were well understood. Measures were designed primarily to dampen the social impact of unavoidable unemployment; by offering benefits and cash transfers unrelated to work, it was hoped that the pain involved with the inevitable reduction in labour supply could be mitigated. Some of these measures – notably early retirement – were implemented without much consideration of potential future costs.

Such interventions, justified by equity and solidarity, can conflict directly with the objective of efficiency during the transition. For example, it is well known that, at least in the medium to long term, the transition implies a unprecedented reallocation of economic activity. Table 4.1 shows the massive shift of relative activity that has already occurred in these countries. In addition to a shift towards services, there was also a marked shift out of agriculture in some countries, notably Poland and Hungary; in Bulgaria and Romania, agricultural activity increased in both relative and absolute terms. Assuming that elasticities of employment are comparable to those observed in industrial economies, there is room for optimism that employment growth in services (with the possible exception of Hungary, which has had a longer transition than the other countries), will re-employ some of the 4.5 million jobless.

One of the greatest challenges facing the CEE countries is to develop a system of social insurance that guarantees basic needs of the population without impeding labour mobility necessary for a successful transition. Inter-industry and occupational shifts necessitate significant redeployment of talents and skills, and are associated with potential losses of human capital and reductions of expected lifetime income. Despite abun-

Table 4.1 Changing structure of output and employment in CEE economies, 1989–95

	Percentage points change in share of:	
...originating in	GDP	Employment
Agriculture		
Bulgaria	+2.0	+3.9
Czech Republic**	−0.7	−5.1
Hungary*	−3.7	−9.8
Poland*	−5.6	−7.0
Romania*	+6.2	+12.4
Slovakia	+0.1	−4.6
Slovenia*	+0.2	na
Industry		
Bulgaria	−28.0	−8.0
Czech Republic**	−14.9	−4.0
Hungary*	−2.7	−9.6
Poland*	−11.9	−3.4
Romania*	−20.5	−14.1
Slovakia	−27.1	−7.4
Slovenia*	−9.2	na
Services		
Bulgaria	+26.0	+4.0
Czech Republic**	+14.2	+9.1
Hungary*	+6.4	+22.4
Poland*	+17.5	+10.4
Romania*	+14.3	+1.7
Slovakia	+27.0	+19.2
Slovenia*	+9.1	na

*1989–1994
**1991–1995
***1990–1995
Sources:
GDP: EBRD (1996) *Transition Report*; CERGE (1997).
Employment: EC (1992, 1995). OECD-CEET database; EC (1995), Service Sector: EC (1992)

dant anecdotes of highly paid engineers who took to driving taxis and waiting on tables, sectoral and occupational transitions are costly, especially when irreversibilities are involved. By reducing the cost of not acting, out-of-work benefits can increase the option value of waiting, and thereby the implicit cost of mobility. At the same time, benefits serve the important function of cushioning adjustment to systemic change and will be essential for maintaining political support of further restructuring. Moreover, the 'entitlement' effect – that employment is necessary to gain access to some social benefits – increases the value of jobs and could induce young, otherwise ineligible workers to accept work in expanding sectors. Unemployment benefits and labour supply reducing measures also allow for faster restructuring insofar as social acceptance of job cuts is enhanced.

Policies should also avoid impeding within-industry mobility of production factors required for a successful transformation. As is well known from the US context, heterogeneity of firms is present even within fine industrial classifications, with succeeding and expanding while others contract or fail at the same time.[2] Mobility of both capital and labour among alternative uses is costly even in unregulated markets; policies should be avoided which make such redeployment of productive resources more costly and time-consuming. Just as policy-makers actively support the development of a national capital market, they could implement a number of policies supporting a national labour market. For example, governments should reduce mobility-inhibiting aspects of housing regulations and poor transport infrastructure (roads, bridges, rail and bus lines). Another useful policy has been the computerization of the public employment services (PES) in order to facilitate information exchange on vacancy availability, as was done in Bulgaria, the Czech Republic, and Slovakia early on in the transition. A third example is to break the linkage between firms and provision of social benefits, which is especially widespread in Russia (Commander and Schankerman, 1997).

It is to be expected that, with the introduction of market incentives, labour market participants will be confronted with a trade-off between benefits and costs of labour force participation. The socialist goal of work for all at all costs was inefficient because it evidently ignored preferences for other activities: leisure, family, household production (especially the raising of children), as well as retooling for future activities. In the past 7 years of transformation, the CEE countries have experienced dramatic declines in labour force participation rates (Chapter 2). Male labour force participation has fallen below levels in Western Europe, while female participation – even after a sharp decline – remains relatively high. *The high relative labour force participation of females relative to males is one of the most striking features of labour markets in transition.* Often cited as contributing factors are the superior day-care facilities, maternity leave and greater access to male-dominated occupations under socialism. Perhaps more important is a ratchet-effect which is often observed in labour supply behaviour. In a celebrated paper, Clark and Summers (1982) showed that the cohort of US American young women drawn into the labour supply during the World War II was reluctant to return to inactivity afterwards, and exhibited participation rates markedly higher than cohorts before or afterwards. Whether this effect stems from habit formation or the accumulation of human capital is unclear; in any case, this fact has important ramifications for the composition of CEE labour supply.

Regardless of its causes, this fact has probably given these countries a more efficient (and progressive) allocation of human resources, considering the current bias towards 'female' skills.[3] On the other hand, it seems imperative for policy-makers to ascertain the extent to which disincentives for both male and female participation are linked to the provision of social benefits and other institutions.

4.1.2 Out-of-Work Benefits and the Tightening of Unemployment Benefits

As a result of the sudden collapse of labour demand, most initial income support in the transformation was provided by national systems of unemployment insurance and benefits; in order to assess their effects on work incentives and labour-force participation, it is necessary to describe their recent evolution. Introduced at the start of transition, unemployment benefit systems reflected both social insurance and social assistance principles and allowed for nominal replacement rates as generous as in many OECD countries. Over time, chronic inflation and incomplete indexation of ceilings eroded unemployment benefits to levels close to the minimum wage with little direct relation to previous contributions.

Yet it was ongoing budgetary crises and consolidation efforts – and not allocative efficiency arguments – which forced public authorities to tighten eligibility and reduce potential benefit duration. Maximum duration was halved in the Czech Republic, Slovakia and Hungary, and a maximum duration of one year was set in Poland (where it had previously been open-ended). Gross statutory replacement rates were cut in Bulgaria and in the former Czechoslovakia; in Poland, the earning-related system was turned into a flat-rate scheme. The lifting of benefit minima or the introduction of benefit ceilings ranging between 140% and 150% of the minimum wage also contributed to reducing benefit levels. In the Czech and Slovak Republics, regulatory changes were applied to all current recipients, while in Bulgaria, Poland and Hungary existing entitlements continued to be honoured. The tightening of benefits hit the long-term unemployed (with incomplete spells of greater than one year) especially hard, and the result was a sharp decline in the proportion of registered jobseekers receiving unemployment benefits.[4] The burden of supporting these individuals generally fell onto social assistance schemes. These programmes generally involve a means-test and require additional resources to administer, especially under conditions of systemic transformation – i.e. with poor tax records and a large underground economy.

These abrupt policy changes have generated useful information on the effect of benefits on job take-up. With the exception of the Czech

Republic – which is due as much to plentiful vacancies as the nature of benefit administration there – flows from unemployment to employment have not increased appreciably; at the same time, reduced duration of benefits resulted in larger flows from unemployment to non-participation.[5] This is confirmed not only by the declining proportion of outflows to jobs as a percentage of total outflows from registered unemployment in most countries (Boeri, 1996b), but also by evidence from matched labour force survey data, which can better discriminate between unemployment and inactivity. These figures point to a marked increase in the proportion of flows to non-participation originating from an unemployment spell compared to those coming directly from employment.

4.1.3 Differences Between Headline (Registry) and Labour Force Survey Unemployment

Because virtually all CEE countries insist on reporting unemployment based on registry data, it is necessary to ask about the nature of this unemployment. Some evidence on the importance of these incentives and the nature of unemployment is now available from comparisons of survey and registry unemployment. With the support of international organizations, unemployment estimates based on survey data and ILO standards are now conducted regularly in most CEE economies, and are widely used in research for assessing joblessness there. It is agreed among labour economists that these data provide the closest approximation to what is generally referred to as effective labour supply, as it measures the self-reported activity of employable individuals who are fit and available for work. Using this metric, worker discouragement reflects an assess-· ment that work at current wages and job availability is not an economically viable strategy.

Registry unemployment, in contrast, is based on actual count data gathered at local labour offices. The incentive to register at the labour office is contingent on net advantages provided by labour offices. These include access to employer information, job counselling and manpower training programmes; at the same time, registration is not only a precondition for eligibility for unemployment benefits, but also in some countries for free health insurance, and a number of other benefits.[6] The relationship of registry to survey unemployment can be viewed as an indicator of these relative incentives. Table 4.2 shows that this ratio deviates widely from country to country. In countries where it is significantly less than one, job information services and social benefits linked to employment offices are relatively unattractive or difficult to qualify for.[7] Values in excess of unity suggest that either that many registered have

Table 4.2 Survey versus registry unemployment and benefit receipt in 1995 (000s)

Country	Registry unemployment	Survey unemployment	As a fraction of survey unemployment:		
			Registry unemployment	Unemployment benefit recipients	Registered U social asst. recipients
Czech Republic	155.0	189.0	0.82	0.12	0.27
Hungary	507.7	416.5	1.22	0.38	0.47
Poland	2694.6	2276.8	1.18	0.54	na
Romania	1111.3	967.9	1.15	0.21	0.77
Slovakia	348.2	324.5	1.07	0.27	0.49
Slovenia	121.5	70.0	1.74	0.40	0.08

Source: OECD-CEET Database.

ceased to search, or that continued registration is a requirement for other benefits administered by the employment offices. It may be important to ask whether the latter reflects efficient use of employment agency resources.[8]

4.1.4 Benefit Cuts, Social Net and the Poverty Trap

One of the greatest challenges in the transformation is to develop a system of social insurance that guarantees the basic needs of the population, without unduly impeding labour mobility. Chapters 2 and 3 have taken note of the relatively low level of mobility observed in the CEE countries. This applies not only to firm-to-firm transitions, but also to unemployment transitions which are due both to sluggish labour demand as well as the readiness to accept employment opportunities implying wage cuts.

Recent tightening of unemployment benefits, while intended to reduce unemployment durations, may ultimately weaken incentives to take up jobs at the lower end of the wage distribution. Table 4.2 shows that unemployment benefits now reach only a fraction of the unemployed, while social assistance has taken up the slack. Social assistance is conditional on passing a means test and is usually associated with a near 100% marginal tax rate on earned income. As in OECD countries, no-earner households and unemployed in households with numerous children are likely to fall into unemployment and poverty traps as a result of the shift to social assistance (see Gregg and Wadsworth, 1995 for evidence on the UK). Moreover, social assistance benefits are typically of unlimited duration and PES administrations have neither means nor incentives to enforce work-tests receiving income transfers. Because social assistance is generally paid out of general government revenues with significant involvement of local administration budgets, a shift from unemployment insurance to social assistance tends to reduce burdens on extra-budgetary funds financing unemployment benefits, active policies and the PES administration.

Measured relative to average wages in the economy, generous benefit systems tend to depress incentives for accepting low-paying jobs in otherwise expanding sectors – for example, services. This is especially true if job losers come from better paying traditionally industrial sectors and possess high levels of firm and industry-specific human capital. While comprehensive evidence on these shifts is not currently available, it is certainly one interpretation of the long durations observed in the CEE countries. As in the United States and the UK, reemployment in the CEE countries following involuntary separations can be associated with significant wage cuts for some groups (Orazem et al. 1995; Köllő and Nagy, 1996).

As already discussed in Chapter 2, unemployment benefits have become less and less important over time, as they converge to minimum levels and eligibility declines. Table 4.2 shows that only in Poland and Slovenia do more than a third of the unemployed receive unemployment benefits. At the same time, coverage of social assistance has increased. This shift to social assistance carries with it a number of difficulties. First it relies heavily on means- (and hence family-) testing. It is notoriously difficult to deal with these disincentives, and this problem becomes even more acute when the structure of earnings is compressed. The relevance of the emerging poverty trap is given by Table 4.3, which compares the social assistance levels with wages.

4.2   Active Labour Market Policies

4.2.1   *Justification During the Transition*

Active labour market policies (ALMPs) are designed to facilitate reintegration of identifiable groups which tend to dominate long-term unemployment. ALMPs are usually classified into three types.[9] *Job intermediation* aims at improving information about vacancy availability, qualifications currently in demand, and future prospects. Especially in emerging, transforming economies, the establishment of labour exchanges assist in overcoming congestion externalities, or exploiting scale economies in matching. Labour offices also provide guidance to

Table 4.3   Social assistance and the wage distribution, 1994

Country	Social assistance benefits (a) as a percentage of:		
	Minimum wage	Low pay (b)	Average wage
Bulgaria (c)	86.7	57.3	35.2
Czech Republic	98.1	49.0	31.3
Hungary	64.8	34.3	20.4
Poland	86.0	59.2	33.8
Slovak Republic	81.0	46.6	31.5
Slovenia	–	56.2	32.7

Notes: (a) Bulgaria: minimum income; Czech and Slovak Republics: minimum subsistence level; Hungary: 80% of the social pension; Poland and Slovenia: minimum pension.
(b) Two-thirds of the median wage.
(c) 1993.

Sources: OECD-CCET Labour Market Database for data on wages; national sources for data on social assistance benefits.

the unemployed and help solve moral hazard problems involved in job search through monitoring and administration of unemployment insurance and assistance.

Labour market training measures are designed to improve worker skills, but are justified only to the extent that workers lack access to capital markets to finance human capital investments themselves, or that markets for education do not function properly. In the context of systemic transformation, it might also be the case that firms provide too few general skills and too much specific training relative to the socially optimal level. Since borrowing against future income is difficult even in economies with advanced capital markets, a rationale for training programmes exists, assuming skills are created which are in excess demand.

Job creation schemes – either direct make-work or employment subsidies – usually comprise the largest component of ALMPs and are aimed at increasing the demand for labour, particularly for those individuals in long-term unemployment. Such interventions are often rationalised if workers are 'scarred' by unemployment or discriminated against ('ranked') because of their current spell of joblessness. According to this argument, current employment status is a noisy signal of worker quality.[10] State job creation programmes may jam the negative signal of unemployment to employers, and to the extent the signal is inefficient (a false positive: that the individual in question merely had bad luck) could improve welfare. In a transformation context, in which all firms are shedding excess labour and selecting their least desirable productive employees for culling, this interpretation seems plausible. Another interpretation of job creation schemes is a test of the unemployed's willingness to work, as they are usually used to generate offers for long-term unemployed (Jackman, 1994; OECD, 1996b). In general, targeted job creation for problem groups can increase outflows out of unemployment and reduce the power of insiders to block downward adjustment of real wages.[11]

Since the onset of the transformation, the message from the OECD and other international organizations been to maintain and expand ALMPs. As a result, CEE countries have set up a large porfolios of ALMP programmes and have received consistent praise for their swift implementation of these measures. Table 4.4 provides an overview of these data. It shows that a wide divergence has opened up between those who which spend large amounts per inflow into these programmes (Czech Republic, Hungary) as opposed to the more frugal countries (Bulgaria, Poland, Slovakia and Slovenia). At the same time, another gap has emerged between those countries which spend relatively little on passive measures overall (Bulgaria, Czech Republic and Slovakia) and those spending large amounts (Poland, Slovakia Slovenia, and especially Hungary). A large

Table 4.4 An overview of active and passive unemployment policies in CEE economies

Country	Active measures			Passive measures		
	Total active spending (% of GDP)	Total inflows to programmes (% of labour force)	ALMP expd. per % point LF inflow (% of GDP)	Total passive spending (% of GDP)	Unemployment rate, % (LFS)	GDP cost per % point unemployment
Bulgaria (1993)	0.09	0.6	0.15	0.67	21.4 (1993:III)	0.03
Czech Republic (1993)	0.20	0.8	0.25	0.16	3.8 (1993:III)	0.04
Hungary (1993)	0.67	3.4	0.12	2.27	12.0 (1993:III)	0.19
Poland (1993)	0.36	5.7	0.06	1.82	13.1 (1993:III)	0.14
Slovakia (1993)	0.44	4.0	0.11	0.77	12.7 (1993:III)	0.06
Slovenia (1995)	0.68	11.0	0.06	0.75	7.4 (1995:II)	0.10
Sweden (1993–4)	2.98	15.2	0.20	2.77	9.7 (1993–4)	0.07
Spain (1994)	0.60	2.2	0.27	3.26	23.8 (1994)	0.14
UK (1993–4)	0.57	2.4	0.24	1.60	10.0 (1993–4)	0.16

Source: OECD (1996a) *Employment Outlook*, authors' calculations.

component of the difference here can be explained by differing unemployment incidence (and hence the number of benefit claimants) in the various countries.

4.2.2   Lingering Doubts

While the intention of active labour market policy is admirable and has considerable political support among both the employed and the unemployed, a strong case can also be made that ALMPs have *negative* effects on the functioning of labour markets. Drawing to some extent on the Swedish experience, Calmfors (1994) adduces evidence that ALMPs can operate quite inefficiently, benefiting those who would be hired anyway or inducing offsetting behaviour by employers elsewhere; under such conditions, ALMPs are a questionable use of public resources. At the same time, some evidence supports programmatic targeting of problem groups as a means of getting around this problem (OECD, 1993).

Overall evidence on ALMP effectiveness on individual re-employment prospects is mixed, and scepticism concerning the efficacy of active labour market policies has increased in recent years.[12] European commentary has focused on the unsuccessful response of Swedish and Finnish labour markets to shocks since 1990, in stark contrast to the 1970s and 1980s, when low unemployment in Nordic economies was widely attributed to high spending on ALMPs. In the aftermath of the recessions of the early 1990s, both countries now have open unemployment several times higher than levels prevailing in the 1970s and 1980s, and both show no sign of returning to previous levels. Active labour market policies have done little to reverse this development, and may be incapable of doing so under conditions of high unemployment.[13]

The microeconometric evidence from Hungary and Poland – two countries where preliminary evaluations of active labour market policies are available – is also negative. Training course participation tends to be offered to jobseekers with favourable labour market characteristics (Micklewright and Nagy, 1994) and who would have found jobs anyway. Participation in public works schemes also ostensibly reduces the probability of finding a regular job (Puhani and Steiner, 1996), suggesting a stigma attached to participation in these programmes. These problems are exacerbated in transition economies by poor signal value of educational attainment and previous experience and by the context of transition, which makes it more difficult to predict the skill requirements of the new jobs being created (Boeri, 1997a).

4.2.3 Active Labour Market Policy in the Czech Republic: Model or a Fair Weather Friend?

After six years of transformation, the Czech Republic remains an outlier in the labour market experience of transition economies. Its unemployment – which remained under 4% from the start of transition until mid-1997 – remains the envy of the OECD as well as the transforming economies, and youth unemployment was roughly 6.5% in mid-1996, compared with about 9% in Germany, 20% in Sweden and 40% in Spain.[14] It is tempting to link the unemployment success of the Czech Republic to its implementation of active labour market policies (ALMP), and a number of successful aspects of Czech active labour market policy have been isolated by researchers.[15] These include 'carrot and stick' administration of benefit, subsidies targeted towards additional job creation for young, unskilled, and long-term unemployment, and a well-organized network of employment offices which actively supervise and assist workers.[16]

It is nevertheless difficult to construct a convincing case for the Czech model, especially since the economy is unusual in a number of respects, and other circumstances peculiar to the Czech Republic may in fact be responsible for the 'unemployment miracle' (OECD, 1995a). These include favourable initial conditions with respect to industrial specialization, a well-trained labour force, a large potential for service employment (tourism especially), a tradition of entrepreneurship, a small agricultural sector, and proximity to Germany with its demand for low wage labour and low-cost production sites. Less optimistic observers cite the minimal restructuring which has taken place in privatized state enterprises as a sign that storms lurk on the horizon; recent bank failures and growing internal and external macroeconomic imbalances in the Czech Republic do not belie this impression.

Direct evidence for the effectiveness of ALMP on unemployment can be obtained by studying the Czech and Slovak Republics in the years following the velvet revolution and the velvet divorce (the dissolution of Czechoslovakia). Until 1993, the two countries shared a labour market law introduced in 1991 which was applied – on paper at least – uniformly throughout the Czech and Slovak Federation.[17] The fact that Slovakia experienced a sharper rise in unemployment in the years 1991 and 1992 means that it also experienced a disproportionate budgetary burden for passive labour market expenditures. On 1 January 1993, the federation split into two independent entities, with the consequence that a large budget imbalance emerged in the Slovak Republic. This was soon followed by significant cuts in ALMP spending per unemployed in 1993 and thereafter; the effects of these cuts were exacerbated by the sharp rise in unemployment.

One fact that arises from the difference between the Czech and Slovak experiences is that ALMP programmes were modest in both spending per person and relative to the size of the labour force. *In this direct sense, they alone cannot explain the difference between Czech and the Slovak unemployment rates.* Rather, job subsidies and job creation ALMPs seem to have a multiplier effect on the supply of private vacancies. Just as important, the make-work scheme (Publicly Useful Jobs, or PUJ) seems to provide an important screening mechanism for testing readiness to work and thereby determining the eligibility for unemployment benefits.[18] Indeed, there is econometric evidence of a modest effect of ALMPs on flows from unemployment to jobs in the CEE economies.[19] This impact is robust whether measured by spending, inflows of positions created or take-up of such positions. By focusing on aggregate outcomes, the approach accounts for substitution between unemployed participants and non-participants, as well as the possibility that even temporary reductions in unemployment claimants can affect job matching by freeing employment service staff and resources for job placement activities. It is less able to account for substitution effects – for example, the extent to which employers intentionally increase turnover to qualify for such subsidies.[20]

Viewed in this light, the use of ALMPs to increase turnover can be interpreted as accepting some inefficiency (in the form of displacement) as the price of 'churning up' stagnant pools of unemployed. In the context of the Czech/Slovak comparison, Burda and Lubyova (1995) show that the Slovak unemployment rate would have been 8.6% in 1992 rather than 12.5%, had Slovakia been able to maintain Czech outflow rates during that year, which was related in part to high ALMP flows (3% of the labour force). Conversely, had the Czech Republic outflow rates been at Slovak levels, its unemployment rate would have been 8.0%. Using a panel of Czech district data, Boeri and Burda (1996) estimate ALMP 'multipliers' on flow data in excess of unity, or that an outflow into an ALMP position has an effect on outflows into private employment. This can be explained by a pure matching effect – high vacancy reporting by employers to obtain subsidies leads to improved services for the unemployed. Alternatively, the effect of increased PES staff time for those remaining in the register enhances job matching, while this effect falls to zero with increasing case loads.[21] As evidence for this effect, Boeri and Burda (1996) report a statistically significant association of PES staff on outflows from unemployment in a cross-section of Czech labour market offices. In particular, a 1% increase in counselling staff is associated with 0.2% more outflows out of registered unemployment into regular (i.e. not make-work) employment. It is interesting that this effect is not present for staffing directly associated with active labour market policy such as training. This is consistent with evidence from other countries (Lehmann, 1993; OECD, 1993).

4.2.4 Limits to ALMPs

Experience in the Czech Republic suggests that stricter benefit administration is most successful in promoting flows from unemployment to jobs when flanked by wide-scale implementation of active labour market policy programmes. The two measures can be self-reinforcing. Large inflows into active programmes substitute for a lack of vacancies and temporarily boost outflows to jobs, even during periods of low economic activity. Reduction of the entitlement period stimulates take-up of subsidized jobs, while active labour market programme involvement enhances the effectiveness of job search also for those with more difficult re-employment prospects. Although much work still remains to be done in evaluating the costs and benefits of ALMPs, one tentative lesson of the Czech experience is that interactions between active and passive policies should be exploited when possible by policy-makers. This is important, as the two spheres are often treated separately in OECD countries and sometimes managed by different administrations.

In any case, the maintenance if not further development of active labour market programmes should be a priority for the CEE economies. As Table 4.5 shows, there has already been substantial progress in implementing job creation, training and targeted programmes, with most countries focusing on subsidized employment. Global subsidies, while preferable to training in that they allow a larger role for market influences, tend to be expensive and it might be worth shifting resources into selective subsidies as these economies begin to grow again. Focus should continue on improving placement services (possibly via competition with private placement agencies). There may be further potential for promoting regional mobility, although – as shown in Chapter 2 – without fundamental improvements in infrastructure, this will have its limits.

Recent experience in some Nordic economies suggest that reliance on high staffing levels and intensive supervision of the unemployed can be an Achilles heel in the face of large negative shocks.[22] For labour offices to prevent the labour market to high-unemployment equilibria, an aggressive expansion of staffing is necessary; in order to maintain a carrot-and-stick policy, it would necessitate an increase in funding for job creation and subsidy. This argument has particular relevance for the Czech 'employment miracle', which is often cited in support of their implemen-

Table 4.5 Detail on active and passive unemployment policies in CEE economies (in percent of GDP)

Country	Active measures					Passive measures	
	PES	Labour market training	Subsidized employment	Measures for disabled	Youth measures	Unemployment benefits	Early retirement
Bulgaria (1993)	0.07	0.01	–	–	–	0.67	–
Czech Republic (1993)	0.11	0.01	0.04	0.01	0.03	0.16	–
Hungary (1993)	0.16	0.11	0.29	–	0.11	2.16	0.11
Poland (1993)	0.02	0.03	0.19	0.04	0.08	1.67	0.15
Slovakia (1993)	0.11	0.03	0.27	0.02	0.02	0.55	0.22
Slovenia (1995)	0.13	0.08	0.36	0.04	0.07	0.75	–
OECD (1994)	0.10	0.20	0.10	0.10	0.10	1.00	0.10
EU and EFTA (1994)	0.20	0.30	0.20	0.20	0.20	1.80	0.20

Source: OECD (1996a) *Employment Outlook,* OECD (1997).

tation of ALMPs. A similar situation seems to prevail there as in Sweden in the 1970s and early 1980s. In the years 1991–3, while the Slovak spending was declining, spending in the Czech Republic for ALMPs was increased sharply. In later years these expenditures were curtailed suggesting a large amount of flexibility. While Slovak employment agencies increased staffing by 40% over the period 1991–3, this was insufficient to prevent an increase in the case load per staff member from 83 to 112. At the same time the Czech case load declined from 50 to 32 (Burda and Lubyova, 1995). It is tempting to conclude that initial conditions plus the flexibility of Czech labour market policy was a distinguishing feature differentiating the two countries.[23] This has the troubling implication that future shocks to the Czech economy may – as was the case of Sweden – lead to persistent increases in unemployment, unless the PES is able to act flexibly and aggressively in response.

4.3   Taxes, Regulations and the Underground Economy

4.3.1   *Taxation and the Fiscal-Unemployment Trap*

The collapse of central planning meant relinquishing control over large parts of the economy to private owners and managers. An unfortunate by-product of this episode was that as many revenue sources disappeared, governments were forced to increase taxation of wages, either directly or via 'contributions' to various social funds. Because these taxes and contributions were initially easier to collect than, say, VAT or income taxes, governments became increasingly dependent on them for revenues. As the early experiences of Hungary and Poland confirm, a key danger faced by policy-makers is the 'vicious circle' of labour taxation and job destruction discussed in Chapters 2 and 3. Generous programmes put in place at the outset of the transition were not expensive because unemployment was negligible. Programme finance and sustainability became problematic only after a rapid rise in unemployment inflated the cost of passive measures (primarily unemployment insurance and assistance), while reducing revenues (as tax collections and contributions decline). As a result, labour taxes were increased, raising labour costs, dampening labour demand and making the system increasingly unsustainable.[24]

Although the literature is agnostic about the role of labour taxation and employment in the OECD (see Nickell and Bell, 1997, or Layard, Nickell and Jackman, 1997), the first panel of Figure 4.1 shows a clear negative association in a cross-section of CEE countries between statutory payroll tax rates on the one hand, and employment ratios on the

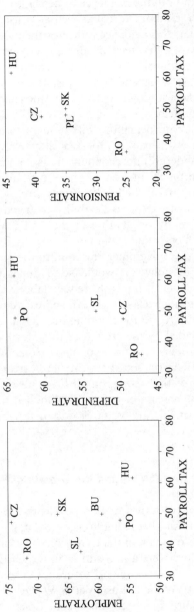

Figure 4.1 Payroll taxes, employment rates and contribution rates. *Source:* Payroll tax rates from EBRD (1995, 1996), OECD Central and Eastern European Database Data are from the CEET database, LF 94:1 and from Boeri (1997b)

other. The second and third panels show that payroll tax rates are positively correlated with both the incidence of dependent individuals (unemployed plus out of the labour force) as well as pensioners in the labour force. Taken together, this evidence indicates the existence of an unemployment/fiscal trap. Under such conditions, a given regime might be consistent with an equilibrium of high job creation, high employment rates, low taxes and low dependency ratios. It could also be consistent with low employment, with high dependency ratios and high labour taxes necessary to finance them.

The elasticity of labour demand, while thought to be relatively low in the short run with given capital stock, is effectively increased by the emergence of the underground economy. It is commonplace for small and medium-sized firms to take on a core of officially reported workers and use a second group 'off the books' in order to reduce tax and social charge liabilities, and to respond flexibility to demand fluctuations. A number of studies, many originating in the CEE countries, confirm a large role for the underground economy.[25]

How should the CEE government respond to the fiscal-unemployment trap? As a matter of policy, it would seem imperative to exploit all available surpluses in social funds, to reduce labour taxation and social contribution rates as much as possible. An aggressive policy of tax reduction could be part of a recipe for avoiding the vicious circle of increasing tax wedges compounded by the growth of the informal economy, which can be attributed primarily to tax avoidance. Some indirect evidence is provided by the OECD on social security tax arrears, which could be regarded as the 'tip of the iceberg' in CEE countries. According to the OECD (1995c), these arrears in Hungary ballooned to 3.7% of tax revenues in 1993, and of this almost 60% was in the form of back social security payments.

4.3.2 Severance Regulations and the Growth of Small Enterprises

An important part of the return to Europe was the adoption of Western European style labour market regulations, for example concerning severance. It became clear early on in the transition that Anglo-Saxon 'hire at will' industrial relations were a non-starter in the CEE countries, as can be readily seen from the overview of severance rules currently in force provided in Table 4.6. While not as strict as Western Europe, these laws are clearly in the spirit of continental regulations. As will be argued below, the accession of these countries to the European Union is likely to mean that these laws will be taken even more seriously or perhaps even strengthened in the future.

Despite evidence from employers' surveys (see Emerson, 1986), economic theory is not unanimous that severance regulation adversely affects employment. In this context, it is useful to distinguish between *severance benefits* paid by the employer directly to the employee, and *severance costs* imposed from the outside on firms for dismissals (formal approval from ministries, adjudication procedures, costs related to 'social plan' regulations, the need for specialized legal staff, etc.). In the former case, wage adjustments or side payments – as long as they are feasible – can generally offset the economic effects of legally mandated severance bonuses.[26] In the case of severance costs representing pure loss or accruing to third parties, however, severance regulation creates a wedge between the wage and the (marginal) productivity of workers.[27] Perhaps it is useful to consider one prominent effect seldom considered in the context of the CEE countries and systemic transformation: the impact of such regulations on small firms and new business formation. It is not surprising that most West European countries have exempted small enterprises from such regulations, although the size threshold has been declining over time. For example, in Germany all enterprises with more than 20 employees have the right to a works council (consisting of three or more members), which must be consulted on a number of matters affecting the workplace.

In a situation of systemic structural change, such regulations could have a non-negligible and possibly severely negative, effect on the transformation.[28] This is because firm formation and dissolution is not only a precondition for production, but performs the important function of processing information, which is still scarce in these economies. Matching of resources, capital, and talents are feasible, but under imperfect information cannot proceed without a certain amount of experimentation.[29] Red tape costs are equivalent to a direct tax on this activity, which curtails gross employment and possibly net growth. In the language of the real options literature (Dixit and Pindyck, 1994), these regulations would increase the value of postponement, and would have unambiguous negative employment effects, to the extent that innovation and technical progress via new firms and new matches of workers and capital do not occur.

By this logic, it would seem important to offer generous exemptions for small firms from these rules, and that 'small' should be liberally defined. This is especially true in light of the fixed cost nature of regulating compliance, for which a separate department and personnel are often required. The enforcement of such rules will either push small enterprises out of business or into the underground economy with consequent impact on tax collection and the fiscal trap discussed above.

Table 4.6   Employment protection regulation in CEE economies

Country	Law	Definition of mass redundancy	Required consultation with employee representatives	Advance notice	Statutory severance pay
Bulgaria	Labour Code 1994 (Ch. 16,1)	Total or partial closing down of enterprise or staff cuts	yes	30–90 days	up to 1 month, more if stipulated in collective agreements or labour contracts
Czech Republic	Labour Code 1993	Redundancies resulting from changing firm objective, new technical equipment, increasing work efficiency, other organizational changes	yes	3 months	2 months' wages unless collective agreements state otherwise
Hungary	Labour Code 1992	Dismissals of 25% of employees or at least 50 people	yes	30–90 days depending on seniority	1 months' pay if job tenure was less than 3 years, up to 6 months' pay if job tenure exceeds 25 years
Poland	Act concerning termination of employment relationships for reasons connected with establishments (1989)	Dismissals of at least 10% of the staff in establishments up to 100 workers or at least 100 workers in establishments employing more than 1000 workers	yes	45 days	1 month's pay for seniority up to 10 years, 2 months' pay for seniority of 10–20 years, 3 months' pay for seniority > 20 years + compulsory allowance for lower income workers in new job, up to 6 months

Romania	Labour Code 1994	Dismissal due to organizational changes, insolvency or reallocation	yes	15 days	at least 3 months' average wages, possibly extended depending on seniority and sector of employment
Slovakia	– Act No. 195/1991, Col. on severance pay after termination of labour contract – Labour Code (Act No. 451/1992 Col.) – Act No. 387/1996 on employment	at least 10 employees in a firm with 20–99 employees, at least 10% of employees in a firm with 100–299 employees, at least 30 employees in a firm with > 299 employees	yes	3 months	2 months' wages, possibly extended up to 5 months' wages on the basis of collective agreement or an internal instruction of the employer
Slovenia	Labour code	Following temporary redundancy of up to 6 months (at reduced pay), no numerical limits	yes	6 months	for employees with at least 2 years' tenure: at least one-half of the wage during the last 3 months, for each year of previous employment

Sources: ILO Labour Law Documents; NatLex (http://natlex.ilo.org); Scarpetta and Reutersward (1994).

4.4　Accession to the European Union and Implications for Labour Market Policy in CEEs

Despite current preoccupation with the single currency project, recent pronouncements from Brussels have not explicitly ruled out EU accession for the CR, Hungary, Poland and Slovenia before 2005. At first sight, admission to the EU would seem to have little to do with labour markets and policy. On the other hand, trade creation and trade diversion will result from integration into the EU pattern of specialization, and this is bound to have effects on the demand for labour. These effects have been addressed in another Economic Policy Initiative volume, and we will have little to say about them here. Yet the process of structural changes implied by integration into the European Union will depend crucially on the flexibility of labour markets, and their ability allocate labour resources efficiently among alternative uses.

Benign neglect of the implications of EU accession would be warranted were it not for the Social Charter of the European Union, which recently achieved renewed respectability after the Blair government signed the UK on. First ratified in Turin on 18 October 1961, the European Social Charter (ESC) has been amended several times, most importantly in October 1991, three decades later. Only in recent years has the EU begun to put teeth into what was initially a platitudinous document. A cursory examination of the provisions of the ESC (and the Additional Protocol of 1988) reveals a number of explicitly guaranteed rights of workers and responsibilities of employers. Table 4.7 reproduces text related to the most important forms of labour market measures implied by the European Charter.

There are two interpretations of the ESC. One is linked to an expression of concern for solidarity for workers in the EU and an effort to enshrine this idea in a common doctrine, which special relevance for newcomers to the club. The 'return to Europe' necessitates, in this view, a common stance on what constitutes 'European' labour market and social policy. The ESC is not a precondition for accession to the European Union, but at the same time it is difficult to imagine that its ratification is irrelevant. Since its original enactment, it has been accepted with little derogation by all countries, and is reasonable to expect that adoption of the Social Charter and the implementation of its principles is implicit in accession to the EU.

A second, more cynical interpretation of the ESC is an attempt to level the competitive playing field by precluding 'wage and social dumping,' meaning preventing poorer member countries which, because of low labour costs and lower standards of living, might offer a cost-competitive production environment.[30] The ESC embodies a number of provisions

Table 4.7 Labour market measures in the European Social Charter

Social welfare European Social Charter (ESC), Turin (1961) I.14	'Everyone has the right to benefit from social welfare services'
Conditions of work (Art. 2) Amendments to the ESC, Strasbourg May 1996	Parties agree to provide: 'reasonable daily and weekly working hours' 'for public holidays with pay' 'for a minimum of four weeks' annual holiday with pay' 'a day of rest' 'that workers performing night work benefit from measures which take account of the special nature of the work'
Severance protection (Art. 24) Amendments to the ESC, Strasbourg May 1996	Parties agree to recognize: 'the right of all workers not to have their employment terminated without valid reasons for such termination connected with their capacity or conduct or based on the operational requirements of the undertaking, establishment or service' 'the right of workers whose employment is terminated without a valid reason to adequate compensation or other appropriate relief.' to ensure: 'that a worker who considers that his employment has been terminated without a valid reason shall have the right to appeal to an impartial body'
Protection from the consequences of Bankruptcy (Art. 25) Amendments to the ESC, Strasbourg May 1996	Parties agree to recognize: 'that workers' claims arising from contracts of employment or employment relationships be guaranteed by a guarantee institution or by any other effective form of protection'
Rights of Workers' Representatives (Art. 28) Amendments to the ESC, Strasbourg May 1996	Parties agree to undertake that workers representatives: 'enjoy effective protection against acts prejudicial to them, including dismissal based on their status or activities' 'are afforded such facilities as may be appropriate in order to enable them to carry out their functions promptly and efficiently'

Source: Council of Europe, European Social Charter (revised); Additional Protocols.

which, taken individually and legalistically, are not specific enough to increase rigidity in the labour market, yet in their entirety they seem to aim at committing member countries to minimal labour standards. Strict implementation of labour regulations and the ESC in general in new member economies would imply loss of export competitiveness for the CEE economies, as well as the chance to develop and raise standards of living rapidly.

Almost all CEE countries have legislation adopting, in principle, the key provisions of the ESC. To a significant extent, this represents an effort on the part of these economies to acquire an 'EU profile' (as in other areas such as agriculture, home affairs, justice, regulation) in the run-up to the accession decision. As Table 4.6 shows, some CEEs already have laws comparable to Western European standards.[31] At the same time, regulations have not been implemented with the vigour observed in members of the European Union, for a number of reasons. The most pressing one is common sense: as long as the recovery of CEE economies from the transition shock remains precarious, flexibility will be required.

The accession issue is also related to the relatively large role played by the informal or underground sector in CEE economies. By definition, employment in the informal sector is unprotected by the rule of law, and implies employment at low wages, firing-at-will, often with little or no entitlement to unemployment insurance, health insurance, or pension contributions of the government. While the underground economy increases welfare for its participants, it also represents a loss of tax revenues for the state, and therefore for Brussels. It also represents a source of labour market flexibility which may not be in the interests of EU members with more restrictive regulations. It may well be in the EU's interest to demand 'West European' restrictions on the informal economy in CEE countries, and thereby measures which inhibit competition along the dimension of wage levels and wage flexibility.[32] Raising wage costs, increasing the option value of the hiring decision, and introducing more regulations and standards will vitiate the attractiveness of central and eastern Europe for direct investment as well as diminish their ability to compete in the internal market. The evidence of Table 4.8 lends credence to this fact: the CEE countries are poor, even on a purchasing power parity basis.

The preceding discussion suggests a potentially negative impact of EU accession on labour market performance. Pressures resulting from accelerated integration (closing of inefficient industries) may be less efficiently managed inside the EU than by countries outside it. To examine this issue, we studied the behaviour of unemployment rates and employment growth for newcomer EU members (those joining after 1970). In particular, we study the behaviour of these variables for Ireland, the United

Table 4.8 GNP per capita, PPP (international dollars)

Country	PPP-GDP per capita	Country	PPP-GDP per capita
Bulgaria	4230	Finland	16390
Czech Republic	7910	France	19820
Slovakia	6660	Germany	19890
Hungary	6310	Greece	11400
Poland	5380	Portugal	12400
Russia	5260	Spain	14040
Romania	2920	Sweden	17850
Slovenia	10014*		

Source: *World Bank Atlas*, 1996.
*WIIW.

Kingdom, Denmark, Greece, Spain, Portugal, Finland, Sweden and Austria around the dates of (1) first application for EU membership and (2) actual accession to the EU, respectively. The unemployment rate is measured relative to a 'core' of long-standing EU members (an unweighted average of Germany, France, and Italy). In order to control for the business cycle, a cyclical component was removed from individual country data using conventional econometric methods.[33] The unweighted average of the results centred around application and accession dates can be seen in the panels of Figure 4.2. While there is no evidence of an average effect of EU accession on employment growth, entry and especially application do seem to be associated with an increase in average unemployment.

To show which countries lay behind the rise in average unemployment, Appendix A reports the corresponding evidence for the individual newcomers. As expected, Spain's experience is particularly coincident with its EU accession, but post-accession Greece and Denmark also experienced striking increases in cyclically corrected unemployment.[34] One interpretation of these findings, which is particularly relevant for Poland and Hungary, is that the accelerated demise of agriculture related to accession was not well managed given the social policies in place at the time. It is especially striking to note that Portugal, in contrast to Spain, did not experience an increase in its unemployment rate. This difference may have been due to wage moderation in the latter following accession, among other things.

Our analysis ignores a number of other factors which may have been in play at the time. In Appendix A we report results of panel regressions which pool data from the above-mentioned countries and take account of other explanatory factors. Application and accession take the form of dummy variables. In our preferred regression, we find a small but statistically significant positive effect of application (0.23%) and accession (0.24%) on unemployment, where these are estimated coefficients on

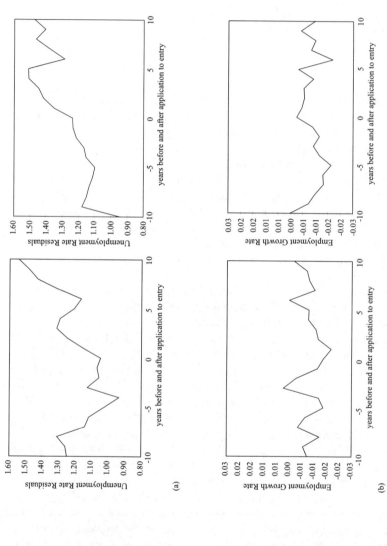

Figure 4.2 Labour market performance for EU newcomers, relative to application and accession dates. (a) Unemployment rate relative to EU-core. (b) Employment growth relative to EU-core

dummy variables. For employment growth, we find a significant and *positive* effect of accession only (0.9%). Overall, the evidence suggests that some countries experience increases in structural or equilibrium unemployment upon application, and that this rise persists after accession. The most likely explanation is the structural change that joining brings is not well-matched to a 'European' safety net in principle designed for wealthy countries.[35] This consideration should be taken seriously in increasing the flexibility of central and eastern European labour markets, that is, the speed by which they adjust to the new economic environment.

4.5   Education Policy

Rising education-specific differentials in wages and employment probabilities documented in the literature and in Chapter 2 are evidence that emerging market economies are in need of substantial investment in general education. This section shows that the gap to be filled by CEE economies is widest at the *secondary level* where enrolment rates are particularly low, structural problems are severe. The policy implication is that social returns to public investment are the highest at this level and steps should be taken without delay to correct this deficit.

4.5.1   Enrolment

Figure 4.3 compares enrolment in all levels of education for each year of age for two CEE countries and OECD. Patterns observed in the Czech and Slovak Republics and Hungary are characteristic of other CEE countries given the basic similarity of their educational systems. The two upper panels show school enrolment as a percentage of the respective age group in 1991 and 1994. In the lower panels, these data are normalized by the average for the OECD. The age-enrolment patterns are almost identical in the two CEE countries, at least after age 16. Enrolment of cohorts attending *higher education* was lower than the OECD average by about 60% in 1991, and 50% in 1994 in both countries. As the chart shows, however, the *major deviation* from the age-enrolment pattern of OECD countries occurs at age 17–20 rather than with the college- or university-aged population. In terms of students attending upper secondary education (within the age group 17–20) the gap seems even wider. At age 19, all enrolled students in the CR and two-thirds of those in Hungary were attending the first or second course of a higher education institution. In contrast, more than half of all students

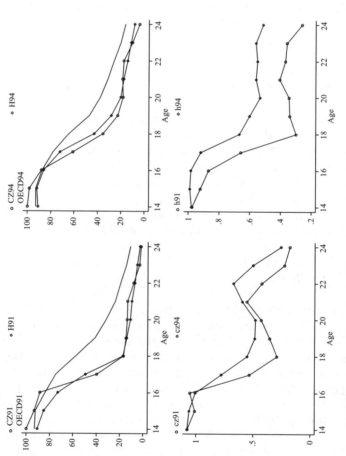

Figure 4.3 Enrolment rates by single year of age in the Czech Republic* and Hungary compared to the OECD average in 1991 and 1994 (*Czech and Slovak Republics in 1991). *Upper row*: enrolment rates; *bottom row*: OECD average = 1. *Sources*: Education at a Glance (1993), tables P13, S8, S9, S10, and (1996) table P3.1., OECD, Paris

enroled in education in the OECD at age 19 attended the final grades of the secondary level.

4.5.2 Structural Bias

The composition of education was heavily biased towards technical manual skills under socialism, and basic vocational or *apprentice schools* continue to account for a high proportion of secondary education. In 1994, vocational and technical programmes accounted for 84% of secondary education in the Czech Republic, and 73% in Hungary, in contrast to a 53% average share in OECD. Combined school- and work-based apprentice schools had 51%, 29% and 19% shares, respectively.[36] The basic vocational schools in the CEE generally provide a part-time general education of inferior quality; in most countries training in apprentice schools fails to conclude in a 'maturity examination' required for higher education studies.

4.5.3 Returns to Education

Public efforts at expanding the secondary level of education are justified on the basis of rate-of-return calculations.[37] Figure 4.4 summarizes estimations by Varga (1997) of private and social returns during the transition in Hungary. The results confirm our claims above that the highest social returns are achieved in general secondary education. The enormous gap between the social and private rates in the case of higher education indicate that a great deal of public support is converted into private benefits by university graduates.

While these results apply only to Hungary, the reasons behind the cross-sectional and time-patterns discovered by her study seem generally valid in the CEE region. The gap between private and total costs is narrower in secondary education partly because higher education is more costly; this is a basic reason but some further important, region-specific differences exist. Secondary school pupils in CEE typically do not receive public financial support while university students typically do. Teenagers usually live with their parents in these countries, so their expenses are financed privately. In contrast, many university students pay publicly subsidized prices for accommodation, transport and food. Secondary school students generally do not earn money in part-time jobs, whereas university students do. For these and similar reasons the social and private returns to secondary education are roughly the same, their dynamics are primarily governed by changes in relative wages and

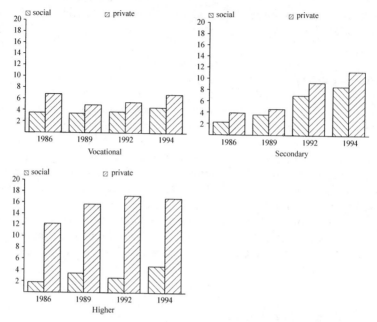

Figure 4.4 Social and private rates of return to education (Hungary, 1986–94). *Source*: Varga (1996). Drawn using data from Tables 5 and 9 with the permission of the author.

unemployment rates, and they tend therefore to move in tandem. In contrast, the gap between private and social returns may be substantial in higher education, and the evolution of wages may not be a good predictor of the social benefit from colleges and universities.

Despite great efforts made by CEE governments (and households) to expand secondary education, the gap has not yet been closed. (See the charts in the bottom row of Figure 4.4.) Also, further efforts are required for eliminating the 'dead-end' character of vocational training. By introducing the technical and economic *lyceé*, Poland and the Czech Republic are attempting to establish an interface between the basic vocational and higher educational levels; apprentice schools in these countries as well as in Romania provide additional courses concluding in maturity examination. The movement to this direction was largely spontaneous and incomplete in Hungary where dead-end basic vocational schools still account for over one-third of 'secondary' education enrolment.

Some observers warn that the expansion of education may increase unemployment since joblessness is particularly high among vocational secondary school leavers. Post-school unemployment rates are largely upwards-biased by the inclusion of young people waiting for next year's university entry examination (rather than for a job). Table 4.9 shows that – as soon as the uncertain period of university entry age is over – general secondary education is highly correlated with job finding probability. The calculations refer to the age groups 16–22 and 22–26 in the stock of Hungarian unemployment insurance recipients in March 1994. Binary logit models are estimated for capturing how education affects the probability of exit to a job. General secondary education has a *negative* impact below age 22: the exit rate is not significantly different from that observed with primary school graduates and lower than in other qualification groups. However, at age 22–26 the likelihood of job finding is already *significantly higher* compared to other secondary qualifications. Obvious caveats apply with the sample used for this estimation but we believe that any model controlling for the disturbances of the immediate post-school period would suggest similar patterns. It might also be mentioned as a weaker supporting argument that there seems to be no connection between youth unemployment and the level, or change, of school enrolment in CEE countries (see EC8, 1995, p. 40).[38]

4.5.4   Implications for Regional Policy

Deteriorating employment prospects and the fall of relative wages for poorly educated workers has hit hard regions with large low-educated populations. Analysing a longitudinal sample of regions, Scarpetta (1995) found that the ratio of the population with primary or lower education

Table 4.9 The probability of leaving insured unemployment for a job. Logit estimates for workers below 22, and those aged 22–26. April 1994, Hungary

	Age < 22		Age 22-26	
	Odds ratio	Z-value	Odds ratio	Z-value
Gender: female	0.6675	−3.926	0.5986	−6.924
Local unemployment rate	0.9778	−3.073	0.9802	−3.940
Education:				
Less than primary	0.8322	−0.166	0.5389	−2.123
Basic vocational	1.4818	4.030	1.4447	4.810
Vocational secondary	1.5232	2.313	1.3923	3.185
General secondary	0.9619	−0.136	1.7476	3.946
Higher	–	–	1.8999	1.905
−Log Likelihood	1415.1		2801.1	
χ(df), Prob > χ^2	49.03	0.0000	109.78	0.0000
McFadden	0.0170		0.0192	
Nobs	2175		4502	

Sample: 10% random sample of UI register, 22 March 1994. Dependent: exit to job during a month. Recall spells excluded. Data source described in Köllő and Nagy (1996).

was correlated with unemployment rates in Poland and Slovakia after controlling for vacancies, proxies of infrastructure, industrial structure and the proximity of Western borders. The coefficient estimated for Hungary was positive but statistically insignificant, probably because of a high level of aggregation (20 regions); in another study, Ábrahám and Kertesi (1996) using data from 170 regions found that the level of education was the single most influential variable among the variables they consider.[39]

The level and composition of skills can particularly strongly hinder the recovery of mono-enterprise or mono-industry regions. Despite this, education reform plays an insignificant role in regional crisis management. Comparing the mining- and steel-dominated regions of Upper Silesia and Borsod, for instance, Fazekas and Gorzelak (1995) mention no coordinated action aimed at this goal in their detailed account of a decade's events. After 10 or 15 years since the crisis began, the often-heard argument that 'restructuring of schooling is a long-term process' has lost considerable credibility. At least five or six cohorts could have completed some kind of a reformed secondary education in these regions since the transformation began.

4.5.5   Implications for Older Workers

The labour market position of 'elderly' workers (age 40 and above) deteriorated markedly in the transition. It is natural to expect that, in response to difficulties in adapting to changing skills requirements, ALMP programmes in CEE countries would pay particular attention to them. While this has happened in some cases – workers above age 50 are given preference in the Czech Publicly Useful Jobs programme – it is not the rule. Hazard rate estimates by Micklewright and Nagy (1994) suggest, for Hungary, that access to training and subsidized jobs sharply declines in age. The return to training declines with age – so workers' demand for retraining falls with age too – but Polish results by Steiner and Kwiatkowski (1995) seem to question whether the explanation is that simple. They compare participation by age groups in self-financed, employer-financed and public retraining schemes in Poland and conclude that older persons are significantly more likely to receive private or self-financed than public training.

In light of the current problems with early retirement and sustainable dependency ratios, the option of retraining elderly workers has received insufficient attention in recent assessments of post-transition ALMPs. Early retirement programmes have dominated all other support schemes, contributing to rather than inhibiting the dis-employment process. The relatively high cost-benefit ratio of education and training courses for older workers militate in favour of on-the-job training and targeted wage subsidy schemes. While schemes reducing the firm's cost of human capital formation in the OECD countries are typically limited to youth programmes, the 'structural break' in the demand for skills in CEE justifies more emphasis on older workers. The precarious situation of government budgets has put severe limits on alternatives, and the labour market prospects of older workers a crucial element in pushing through needed pension reforms. While the effectiveness of ALMP spending may decline as resources are directed towards individuals who learn less efficiently and have shorter remaining life-times to use acquired human capital, such targeting can also be defended on social grounds, i.e. assisting prime age family members facing disemployment and wage loss.

4.6   Conclusion

As the transformation proceeds and formerly centrally planned economies delegate responsibility of resource allocation to markets, they will increasingly resemble and should be considered little different from other less-developed OECD countries or advanced developing economies. This applies especially to the labour market, which allocates the most important resource of all in modern economies; the transition implies, almost tautologically, that the skills and talents of a large fraction of the labour force will have to exhibit some form of mobility, i.e. be reallocated to alternative uses.[40] The optimal speed at which this process occurs is a difficult theoretical question, but, as the transformation continues to gather momentum, will be of vanishing relevance.[41]

The more important questions are arguably those which have been addressed at various points in this monograph: what will be the resting point of these economies, in terms of indicators such as the employment ratio, the participation rate, or labour force turnover? Second, how will labour markets react to future disturbances on the horizon? Finally, how can government policy condition or influence the adjustment process? In particular, can social, employment and education policy contribute to reaching the most appropriate resting point, however defined? Central and East European economies have already been subjected to several severe shocks and accession to the European Union will imply a great deal more to come. This monograph has sought to show that, while the 'return to Europe' is desirable for a number of cultural, historical, and economic reasons, the return need not be unconditional.

Notes

1. Some economists might endorse certain forms of redistribution as policy, if society assigns a sufficiently heavy penalty on inequality and if avoiding it is impossible by other means; interventions of this type will, however, generally imply efficiency costs which cannot be neglected.
2. See Davis and Haltiwanger (1993).
3. The general trend in 'female-friendly' OECD countries (US, UK, Sweden) can be characterized by steadily rising overall participation, which can be decomposed into rapidly rising female and stagnant or declining male participation, especially in the older age brackets.
4. It should be stressed that unemployment benefits for school-leavers were not discontinued, although in Hungary benefits for this group were eliminated. This means that the decrease in coverage rates documented in Table 4.2 cannot be attributed to inflows of large cohorts of jobseekers not eligible to unemployment benefits.
5. See Lubyova and van Ours (1996), and Boeri (1997b).
6. This is the assessment of the OECD in its recent review of the labour market in Slovenia, for example (OECD, 1997a). There, the national employment office pays pension and health insurance contributions for registered reemployed.
7. For example, in the case of Bulgaria and the Czech Republic, durations of benefit are short relative to expected durations.
8. The issue of social welfare versus unemployment benefits is addressed by Boeri (1997b).
9. See Calmfors (1994).
10. See Blanchard and Diamond (1994).
11. See Lindbeck and Snower (1985) and Blanchard and Summers (1986) for elaborations of these ideas.
12. Burtless (1985) reports negative effects of participation in wage-subsidy programmes on reemployment probability, as well as low take-up on the part of employers. Furthermore, macroeconomic effects at the local labour market level may also undo the effects of ALMPs. As Calmfors and Nymoen (1991) and Calmfors (1994) have pointed out, active labour market programmes which guarantee employment set a floor for workers' reservation utility levels, putting upward pressure on wages and raising the natural rate of unemployment. In total, these problems could explain why it is relatively difficult to detect effects of ALMPS empirically. Favourable econometric estimates of the effects of ALMP measures using individual data may reflect selection bias. Because policy often favours the individuals most motivated to search actively, and because internal evaluation procedures often reward successful placement, participants may be chosen for their potential for success rather than need for treatment.
13. For a discussion of the early apparent successes of active labour market policies in the Nordic countries see Jackman, Pissarides and Savouri (1990); for a critical discussion see Calmfors and Nymoen (1991).
14. The Czech miracle is hardly blemished when one takes underemployment and worker discouragement into account (Boeri 1994a).
15. See Boeri (1994a, 1996), Burda (1993), OECD (1995c), Terrell and Munich (1996).
16. Supervision by PES officers can imply better screening and placement of vacancies and job seekers, and possibly lower unemployment. In the Czech Republic, PES placements in 1993–4 accounted for about 50% of total exits from the register to jobs. See Boeri and Burda (1996) for details.
17. This discussion follows Burda and Lubyova (1995).
18. See Terrell and Munich (1996) for an extensive description of eligibility, entitlement and benefit levels in the Czech Republic.
19. See for example OECD (1995c), Munich et al. (1994), Boeri and Burda (1996).
20. Recent evidence relating to experiences of other transforming economies make it clear that conditioning on the country is important for predicting success and may cast doubt on earlier optimism. In particular, the country understudy seems to have a systematic effect on the findings. In Poland, the evidence is almost uniformly negative (Lehmann,

1995; Kwiatkowski, 1996; Puhani and Steiner, 1996) which is often rationalized by poor targeting of programmes (Puhani and Steiner, 1996).

21. See Boeri and Burda (1996).

22. Ljungqvist and Sargent (1995) show in a theoretical search model that endogeneity in monitoring can result in multiple equilibria – one with low unemployment, intensive supervision and monitoring, and high exit rates from unemployment; and another with high unemployment, low monitoring, and low exits from unemployment.

23. It is interesting to note that since 1993, the Czech public employment service has systematically reduced its active policy commitment, presumably because it is presently not needed.

24. A widely-cited case is Hungary. From 1991 to 1993, Hungarian social security contributions rose from 42.3% of wages and salaries to 50.2%. This was a direct result of increasing social insurance burdens and increases in the social security tax contribution rates.

25. See Lacko (1995), who estimates the underground economies of Poland, Hungary and CR as well as more advanced OECD economies on the basis of household electricity use. For a recent review, see EBRD (1995). The extent of the underground economy is not necessarily reflected in employment ratios, of course, since many workers in CEE countries have several jobs, one of them perhaps official, the others in the informal, unreported economy.

26. See, e.g. Lazear (1990) or Burda (1992).

27. The ambiguity arises in part because the way many models are constructed: whether they are general or partial equilibrium; whether costs are lump-sum, linear, or convex; and whether the stochastic environment implies a smooth or discrete evolution of uncertainty. According to available results, severance regulation can have no effects, small effects, or large effects; they can either reduce or increase employment; these effects may depend on whether the costs are large or small. For models in which there can be no effect see Lazear (1990) and Burda (1992), for models in which severance costs can *increase* employment, see Bertola and Bentolia (1990), Bertola (1990); in Bentolila and St. Paul (1993, 1994), Hopenhayn and Rogerson (1993), Bertola and Ichino (1995) severance regulations can reduce employment.

28. This is the message of Hopenhayn and Rogerson (1993).

29. It is for this reason that even in advanced, developed Western economies the amount of churning, that is, the excess of gross labour and job turnover over net changes, or even the excess of labour turnover over job turnover – is enormous. See Burgess, Lane and Stevens (1995) and OECD (1995c).

30. This hypothesis is often voiced by critics of the EU such as Vaclav Klaus.

31. Poland's law is especially noteworthy in that it provides for severance benefits contingent on post-reemployment outcomes (for displaced workers who suffer income losses).

32. This tendency can be observed in the political discussion on enlargement – deepening versus widening. It is significant that the advocates of the former (France, Germany) have more competition to fear than the UK, which has endorsed early EU admission of the CEE countries.

33. Specifically, we estimated the model

$$x_t = \alpha + \Sigma_{i=0,1,2}\beta_i \Delta y_{t-i} + \gamma_1 t + \gamma_2 t^2 + \gamma_3 t^3 + u_t$$

where x is either the OECD standardized unemployment rate or the growth rate of employment, and y is the log of GDP. From the estimates we then constructed and studied the series $x_t - \Sigma_{i=0,1,2} b_i \Delta y_{t-i}$, where the b_i are estimates of the β_i.

34. As the Appendix shows, the newest members of the EU – Austria, Finland and Sweden – have also experienced a rise in joblessness but it is too early to say how much of this is structural. Our results are robust to suppressing these countries from the sample, however.

35. While Baldwin et al. (1997) mention this issue in the introduction to their paper, they do not investigate it directly, as they are concerned with trade and government finance implications of EU accession.

36. See Education at a Glance (1996), OECD, Paris, 123.
37. The *private* rate of return is defined as the discount rate at which the present value of the net income flow that is generated by a particular level of education is equal to the present value of private cost flow associated with that level of education. The *social* return is the rate equalizing the present values of gross earnings and total costs. High private returns may act as a signal for individual 'human capital investors' but for the government the social return has primary importance; the higher the social *relative* to the private return the stronger the case for public support.
38. Youth unemployment rates are the highest in Bulgaria, Poland and Slovakia. The proportion of young people in training was low and decreasing in Bulgaria; high and increasing in Poland; medium-level and stagnant in Slovakia, in and before 1994. [See ECS6 (1994), 24–25.]
39. They used firm density, share of manufacturing, land quality, the share of the Gypsy population and five region dummies. The influence of the Roma ratio was strongest early in the transition but was outweighed by the education effect as early as March 1991.
40. For example, it has been recently noted that two of every three workers in the ex-German Democratic Republic had to be 'mobile' in one sense or another during the transition process.
41. Some examples of work on this question are Aghion and Blanchard (1994), Burda (1993), Castanheira and Roland (1996) and Brixiova (1995).

Appendix A

Labour Market Performance Before and After EU Accession

In this appendix, we elaborate on our analysis of unemployment and employment growth in nine countries before and after accession to the European Economic Community (EEC) or its successor, the European Union (EU).[1] Because candidate countries usually have to 'get their house in order' in order to qualify to join, it is important to distinguish between accession (formal membership) and first application (the lodging of the formal petition for membership). We thus consider both date of the application preceding accession as well as accession as indicators of regime change and as benchmarks for analysing labour market performance. Table A1 provides a timetable of EU accessions and applications to entry. As is evident, the time between application and entry into the EU is variable, ranging from 33 months (Finland) to almost 9 years (Portugal).

Figure A1 displays OECD standardized unemployment rates of those countries. Appendix B provides information to data sources used here. Figure A2 and A3 show 'Burns–Mitchell diagrams' which present 'average' behaviour of unemployment rates and employment growth rates for all countries relative to their respective years of application for membership and of accession. Figure A2 uses unemployment rates relative to the EU15 unemployment rate, whereas for the employment growth rate we used the deviation from the average employment growth rate the EU-core, defined as France, Germany and Italy.[2] Note that German total employment was projected on a time trend, a constant and a dummy variable equal to zero before 1991 and one from 1991 on to eliminate the level shift in the data caused by German unification. The figures suggest that, on average, unemployment rates of candidate countries rose after applying to membership in the EEC. In contrast, EU member-

Table A1 Accessions and applications to entry into the EEC/EU

Country	Date of first application	Date of accession
UK	10.05.1967	01.01.1973
Ireland	10.05.1967	01.01.1973
Denmark	11.05.1967	01.01.1973
Greece	12.06.1975	01.01.1981
Portugal	28.03.1977	01.01.1986
Spain	28.07.1977	01.01.1986
Austria	17.07.1989	01.01.1995
Sweden	01.07.1991	01.01.1995
Finland	18.03.1992	01.01.1995

Source: W. Weidenfels and W. Wessels (eds). *Europa von A-Z*, 5th ed., 1995, Bonn: Europa Union Verlag.

ship seems irrelevant for employment growth, except a small increase in the first years following accession.

Movements in unemployment can also be caused by the business cycle. If countries tended to enter or apply for EU membership at the beginning of a recession, our results could be spurious. To control for cyclical factors, unemployment rates (defined relative to the EU-core unemployment rate) and employment growth rates of newcomer countries were projected on a constant, a current two lags of real GDP growth, and a linear, square and cubic time trend for each country. The sum of the constant, time trends and the regression residuals were used to construct Figures A4 and A5.

The figures confirm the impression of a rising unemployment rate relative to EU-core after application and accession to the EEC, even after controlling for the business cycle. In contrast, the deviation of employment growth to EU-core countries does not show a level shift.

A simple regression analysis confirms the impression from the figures. We estimate a fixed effects model pooling all nine countries into one sample while allowing an individual trend for each country's relative unemployment rate. The specification chosen was

$$\eta_{it}^{(k)} = \mu_i + \tau_{i1}t + \tau_{i2}t^2 + \tau_{i3}t^3 + \sum_{j=0}^{2} \alpha_j g_{it-j} + \beta_1 ap_{it} + \beta_2 ac_{it} + \varepsilon_{it},$$

where μ_i is a fixed effect for the ith country, τ_{in}, $n = 1, \ldots, 3$ are country-specific time trends coefficients, t is a time trend, and g_{it} is the current growth rate of real GDP. The dependent variable is either $\eta_{it}^{(1)} = u_{it}/u_{it}^{core}$ or $\eta_{it}^{(2)} = e_{it} - e_{it}^{core}$, where u_{it} is the unemployment rate and e_{it} is the employment growth rate for the ith country in period t, respectively. The different specifications of the two dependent variables are chosen because e_{it} can take negative values. β_1 and β_2 are the main coefficients

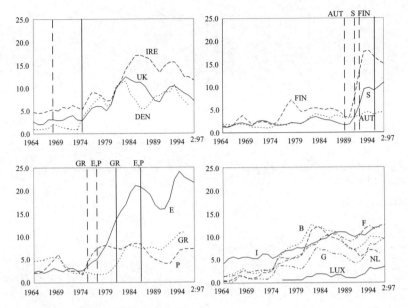

Figure A1   Unemployment rates

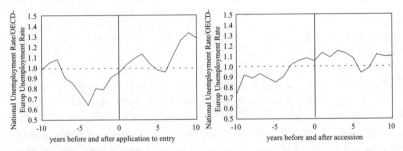

Figure A2   Burns–Mitchell diagrams: unemployment rate relative to EU15 unemployment

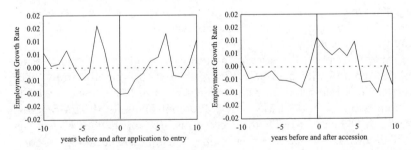

Figure A3   Burns–Mitchell diagrams: employment growth rate (difference from EU-core employment growth rate)

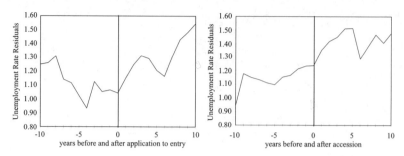

Figure A4 Burns–Mitchell diagrams: cyclically-corrected unemployment rate relative to EU-core

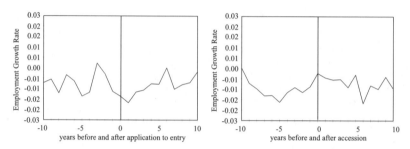

Figure A5 Burns–Mitchell diagrams: cyclically-corrected employment growth (relative to EU-core)

of interest here. $ap_{it}(ac_{it})$ is a dummy variable which takes the value zero before the application (accession) to the EU and one thereafter.

The regression results are presented in Table A2. The cyclical factors show the expected and significant impact, with higher GDP growth associated with lower relative unemployment and higher employment growth. As in the figures, both application as well as accession of a country to the EU is associated with a statistically significantly higher unemployment rate relative to the core. However, in regression (4) where the cubic time trend is omitted, the accession is accompanied by significantly higher employment growth.

Table A3 reports the same specification as Table A2 but includes an 'EMS dummy' with a value of zero before 1978, one afterwards. The results show that relative unemployment rates of EU entrants were significantly higher in the EMS period. But controlling for the EMS period does not change the result that accessions and applications have a significant positive coefficient in the relative unemployment rate regressions. In the employment growth rate regressions the EMS dummy is insignificant.

Table A2 Unemployment and employment growth rate regressions, 1964:1996 (unemployment) and 1966–97/estimate (employment growth)

	$\eta_{it}^{(1)} = u_{it}/u_{it}^{core}$		$\eta_{it}^{(2)} = e_{it} - e_{it}^{core}$	
	(1) linear, square, cubic time trend (not reported)	(2) linear, square time trend (not reported)	(3) linear, square, cubic time trend (not reported)	(4) linear, square time trend (not reported)
Constant	1.926**	1.224**	0.015	−0.006
	(0.362)	(0.206)	(0.038)	(0.016)
g_{it}	−1.764 **	−2.082 **	0.162**	0.172**
	(0.536)	(0.606)	(0.040)	(0.040)
g_{it-1}	−2.796 **	−2.921 **	0.117**	0.122**
	(0.526)	(0.600)	(0.041)	(0.041)
g_{it-2}	−2.827 **	−3.048 **	0.080*	0.084**
	(0.537)	(0.600)	(0.041)	(0.040)
ap_{it}	0.141*	0.204**	−0.004	−0.002
	(0.073)	(0.065)	(0.005)	(0.005)
ac_{it}	0.092	0.225**	0.010*	0.009**
	(0.069)	(0.065)	(0.005)	(0.004)
adj. R^2	0.873	0.838	0.222	0.215
No. of obs.	296	296	288	288

Note: *denotes significance at a 10% level, **at 5%. Standard errors in parentheses.

Table A3 Unemployment and employment growth rate regressions, 1964:1996 (unemployment) and 1966–97/estimate (employment growth) – including EMS dummy

	$\eta_{it}^{(1)} = u_{it}/u_{it}^{core}$		$\eta_{it}^{(2)} = e_{it} - e_{it}^{core}$	
	(1) linear, square, cubic time trend (not reported)	(2) linear, square time trend (not reported)	(3) linear, square, cubic time trend (not reported)	(4) linear, square time trend (not reported)
Constant	1.847**	1.333**	0.014	−0.007
	(0.363)	(0.206)	(0.038)	(0.017)
g_{it}	−1.760 **	−2.013 **	0.162**	0.172**
	(0.533)	(0.596)	(0.040)	(0.040)
g_{it-1}	−2.807 **	−2.880 **	0.116**	0.122**
	(0.523)	(0.590)	(0.041)	(0.041)
g_{it-2}	−2.797 **	−2.897 **	0.080*	0.083**
	(0.535)	(0.592)	(0.041)	(0.040)
ap_{it}	0.140*	0.227**	−0.004	−0.003
	(0.073)	(0.064)	(0.005)	(0.005)
ac_{it}	0.101	0.241**	0.010*	0.009**
	(0.068)	(0.064)	(0.005)	(0.004)
ews_t	0.115*	0.166**	0.002	−0.0003
	(0.059)	(0.052)	(0.004)	(0.004)
adj. R^2	0.875	0.839	0.222	0.212
No. of obs.	296	296	288	288

Note: *denotes significance at a 10% level, **at 5%. Standard errors in parentheses.

Notes

1. For simplicity we shall henceforth refer to all accessions as 'EU accessions'.
2. This was done simply for reasons of data availability.

Appendix B
Data Description

1. Unemployment Rates

   Austria: Standardized unemployment rates, *OECD Quarterly Labour Force Statistics*, 1964–97:2

   Denmark: OECD Economic Outlook, 1960–69, Standardized unemployment rates, *OECD Economic Indicators*, 1979–96

   Finland: Standardized unemployment rates, *OECD Economic Indicators*, 1964–97:2

   France: Standardized unemployment rates, *OECD Quarterly Labour Force Statistics*, 1964–97:2

   Germany: Standardized unemployment rates, OECD Main Economic Indicators, 1964–97:2

   Greece: OECD Economic Outlook, 1960–70, standardized unemployment rates, 1971–95

   Ireland: OECD Economic Outlook, 1960–82, standardized unemployment rates, *OECD Quarterly Labour Force Statistics*, 1983–97:2

   Italy: Standardized Unemployment Rates, *OECD Main Economic Indicators*, 1964–96

   Portugal: OECD Economic Outlook, 1960–70, standardized unemployment rates, *OECD Quarterly Labour Force Statistics*, 1987–97:2

   Spain: Standardized Unemployment Rates, *OECD Main Economic Indicators*, 1964–97:2

   Sweden: Standardized Unemployment Rates, *OECD Main Economic Indicators*, 1965–97:2

   United Kingdom: Standardized Unemployment Rates, *OECD Main Economic Indicators*, 1964–97:2

2. Total Employment: *OECD Economic Outlook*, 1960–97, 1996, 1997(estimates)
3. Nominal GDP: *OECD Economic Outlook*, 1960–97, 1996, 1997: (estimates)
4. GDP Deflator: *OECD Economic Outlook*, 1960–97, 1996, 1997: (estimates)

Appendix C
Burns–Mitchell Diagrams

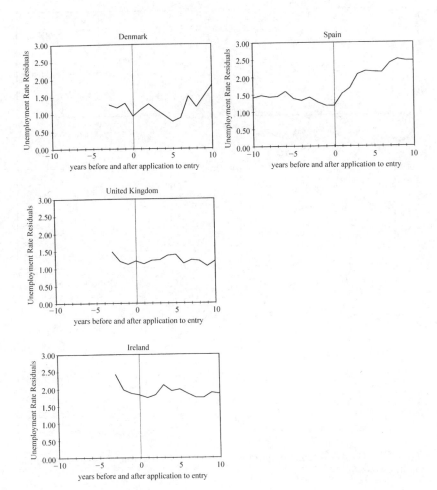

Figure C1 Burns–Mitchell diagrams of relative unemployment rates in individual countries

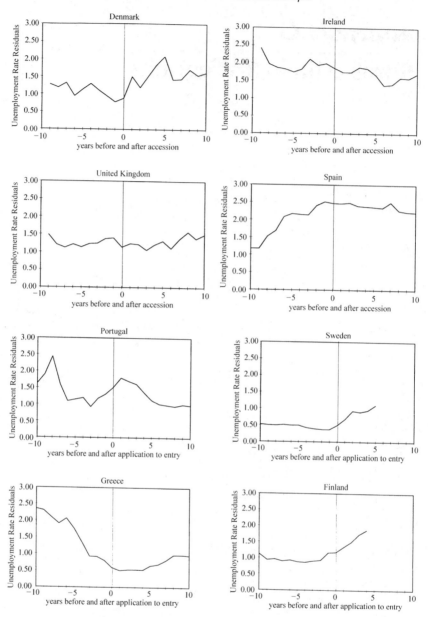

Figure C1 Burns–Mitchell diagrams of relative unemployment rates in individual countries (*contd.*)

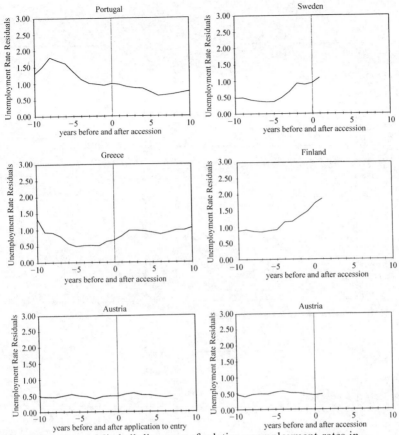

Figure C1   Burns–Mitchell diagrams of relative unemployment rates in individual countries (*contd.*)

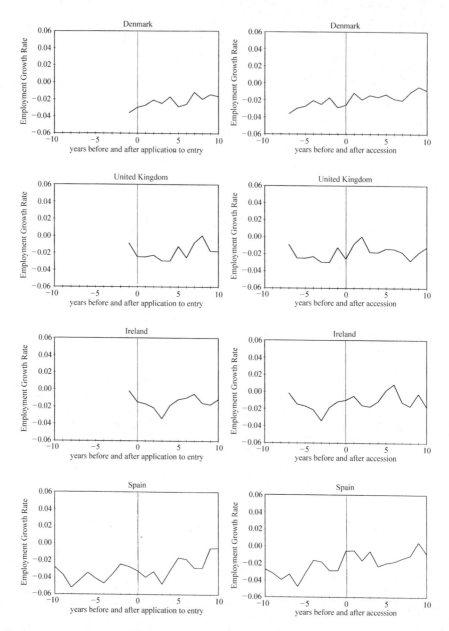

Figure C2   Burns–Mitchell diagrams of employment growth in individual countries

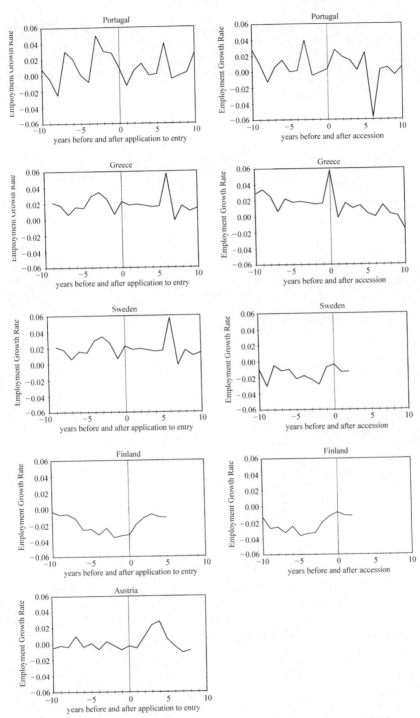

Figure C2 Burns–Mitchell diagrams of employment growth in individual countries (*contd.*)

References

Ábrahám, Á. and Kertesi, G. (1996): 'Regional Unemployment Rate Differentials in Hungary 1990-1995 (The Changing Role of Race and Human Capital)', *Közgazdasági Szemle* 63 (in Hungarian).

Aghion, P. and Blanchard, O. (1994): 'On the Speed of Transition in Central and Eastern Europe', *NBER Macroeconomics Annual* 9.

Andrews, E.S. and Rashid, M. (1996): 'The Financing of Pension Systems in Central and Eastern Europe', World Bank Technical Paper No. 339.

Atkenson, A. and Kehoe, P. (1993) 'Social Insurance and Transition', NBER Working Paper No. 4411.

Baldwin, R, Francois, J. and Portes, R. (1997) 'The Costs and Benefits of Eastern Enlargement: The Impact on the EU and Central Europe,' *Economic Policy* 24.

Basu, S, Estrin, S. and Svejnar, J. (1994): 'Employment and Wage Behavior of Enterprises in Transition', paper presented at the workshop on Enterprise Adjustment in Eastern Europe, Transition Economics Division, Policy Research Department, The World Bank, 22–23 September 1994, Washington DC.

Bean, C. (1989): 'Capital Shortages and Persistent Unemployment', *Economic Policy* 8.

Beleva, I., Jackman, R. and Nenova-Amar, M. (1995): 'Unemployment, Restructuring and the Labour Market in Eastern Europe and Russia', in S. Commander and F. Coricelli (eds.), *Unemployment, Restructuring and the Labor Market in Eastern Europe and Russia*, Washington, DC, World Bank/ EDI.

Benácek, V. (1995): 'Small Businesses and Private Entrepreneurship during Transition', *Eastern European Economics* 33:2.

Bentolila, S. and Saint-Paul, G. (1993): 'The Macroeconomic Impact of Flexible Labor Contracts, with an Application to Spain', *European Economic Review* 36.

Bentolila, S. and Saint-Paul, G. (1994): 'A Model of Labour Demand with Linear Adjustment Costs', *Labour Economics* 1.

Bertola, G. (1990): 'Job Security, Employment and Wages', *European Economic Review* 34.

Bertola, G. and Bentolia, S. (1990): 'Firing Costs and Labor Demand: How Bad is Eurosclerosis?', *Review of Economic Studies* 57.

Bertola, G. and A. Ichino (1995): 'Wage Inequality and Unemployment: US vs Europe', *NBER Macroeconomics Annual* 10.

Blanchard, O.J., Commander, S. and Coricelli, F. (1995): 'Unemployment and Restructuring in Eastern Europe and Russia', in S. Commander and F. Coricelli (eds.), *Unemployment, Restructuring and the Labor Market in Eastern Europe and Russia*, Washington, DC, World Bank/EDI.

Blanchard, O.J. and Diamond, P. (1994): 'Ranking, Unemployment Duration and Wages', *Review of Economic Studies* 61.

Blanchard, O.J., Dornbusch, R., Drèze, J., Giersch, H., Layard, R., and Monti, M. (1986): 'Employment and Growth in Europe: A Two-Handed Approach', in O.J. Blanchard, R. Dornbusch, and R. Layard (eds.), *Restoring Europe's Prosperity*, Cambridge, USA, MIT Press.

Blanchard, O.J. and Summers, L. (1992): 'Hysteresis in Unemployment', in P. Garonna, P. Mori and P. Tedeschi (eds.), *Economic Models of Trade Unions*, London, Chapman and Hall.

Blanchard, O.J. and Summers, L. (1986): 'Hysteresis and the European Unemployment Problem', *NBER Macroeconomics Annual* 1.

Boeri, T. (1994a): 'Transitional Unemployment', *Economics of Transition* 2.

Boeri, T. (1994b): 'Labour Market Flows and the Persistence of Unemployment in Central and Eastern Europe', in *Unemployment in Transition Countries: Transient or Persistent*, Paris, OECD/CCET.

Boeri, T. (1996): 'Unemployment Outflows and the Scope of Labour Market Policies in Central and Eastern Europe', in T. Boeri, H. Lehmann, and A. Wörgötter (eds.), *Lessons from the Experience of Transition Countries with Labour Market Policies*, Paris, OECD.

Boeri, T. (1997a): 'Labour Market Flows in the Midst of Transition', in S. Commander (ed.) *Enterprise Restructuring and Unemployment in Models of Transition*, forthcoming, Cambridge: Cambridge University Press.

Boeri, T. (1997b) 'What Can We Learn from the Experience of Transitional Economies with Labour Market Policies', *Oxford Bulletin of Economic Policy*, forthcoming .

Boeri, T. and Burda, M. (1996): 'Active Labour Market Policies, Job Matching and the Czech Miracle', *European Economic Review* 40.

Boeri, T. and Edwards, S. (1996): 'Long-term Unemployment and Short-term Benefits', paper presented at the OECD-IHS workshop on 'Long-term Unemployment and the Transition from Unemployment Benefits to Social Assistance, Vienna, December.

Boeri, T. and Keese, M. (1994): 'Labour Markets and the Transition in Central and Eastern Europe', *OECD Economic Studies*, No. 18, Paris, pp. 133–63.

Boeri, T. and Oliveira-Martins, J. (1997): 'Transition, Product Variety, and Trade', mimeo, May.

Boeri, T. and Scarpetta, S. (1993): 'Emerging Regional Labour Market Dynamics in Central and Eastern Europe', in S. Scarpetta and A. Wörgötter (eds.), *Regional Dimensions of Unemployment in Transition Economies*, Paris, OECD.

Boeri, T. and Scarpetta, S. (1994): 'Convergence and Divergence of Regional Labour Market Dynamics in Central and Eastern Europe', OECD

Technical Workshop on Regional Unemployment in Central and Eastern Europe, IAS, Vienna, November.

Boeri, T. and Scarpetta, S. (1996): 'Regional Mismatch and the Transition to a Market Economy', *Labour Economics* 3.

Brada, J. and Singh, I.J. (1994): 'Transformation and Labour Productivity in Central and Eastern Europe', paper presented at the workshop on Enterprise Adjustment in Eastern Europe, Transition Economics Division, Policy Research Department, The World Bank, 22–23 September 1994, Washington, DC.

Brixiova, Z. (1995) 'Private Sector Development and Unemployment in Postsocialist Economies', mimeo, University of Minnesota.

Bruno, M. and Sachs, J. (1985): *Macroeconomics of Stagflation*, Cambridge, USA, Harvard University Press.

Burda, M. (1988a): 'Is there a Capital Shortage in Europe?' *Weltwirtschaftliches Archiv* 124.

Burda, M. (1988b): 'Wait Unemployment in Europe', *Economic Policy* 7.

Burda, M. (1992) 'A Note on Firing Costs and Severance Benefits in Equilibrium Unemployment', *Scandinavian Journal of Economics* 94.

Burda, M. (1993): 'Unemployment, Labour Markets and Structural Change in Eastern Europe', *Economic Policy* 16.

Burda, M. (1994): 'Labor Market Institutions and the Economic Transformation of Central and Eastern Europe,' in S. Commander and F. Coricelli (eds.), *Unemployment, Restructuring and the Labor Market in Eastern Europe and Russia*, Washington, DC, World Bank/EDI.

Burda, M. (1995): 'Migration and the Option Value of Waiting', *The Economic and Social Review* 1.

Burda, M. (1996): 'Unemployment in Central and Eastern Europe: East Meets West', in H. Giersch (ed.), *Fighting Europe's Unemployment in the 1990's* Berlin, Springer.

Burda, M. and Lubyova, M. (1995): 'The Impact of Active Labour Market Policies: A Closer Look at the Czech and Slovak Republics', in D. Newbery (ed.), *Tax and Benefit Reform in Central and Eastern Europe*, London, CEPR.

Burgess, S., Lane, J., and Stevens, D. (1995): 'Job Flows, Worker Flows and Churning', CEPR Discussion Paper No. 1125.

Burtless, G. (1985): 'Are Targeted Wage Subsidies Harmful? Evidence from a Voucher Experiment', *Industrial and Labor Review* 39.

Butchikova, A. (1995): 'Have Minimum Wages Hurt Employment in the Czech Transformation?', in G. Standing and D. Vaughan-Whitehead (eds.), *Minimum Wages in Central and Eastern Europe: From Protection to Destitution*, Budapest, CEU Press.

Calmfors, L. (1994): 'Active Labor Market Policy and Unemployment: A Framework for the Analysis of Crucial Design Features', *OECD Economic Studies* 2.

Calmfors, L. and Nymoen, R. (1991): 'Active Labor Market Policies in the Nordic Countries', *Economic Policy* 11.

Carruth, A. and Oswald, A. (1987): 'On Union Preferences and Labour Market Models: Insiders and Outsiders', *Economic Journal* 97.

Castanheira, M. and Roland, G. (1996): 'The Optimal Speed of Transition: A General Equilibrium Analysis', CEPR Discussion Paper No. 1442, July.

CERGE (1997): *Czech Republic: Basic Economic Indicators*, Prague: Centre for Economic Research and Graduate Education.

Chadha, B. and Coricelli, F. (1994): 'Fiscal Constraints and the Speed of Transition', CEPR Discussion Paper No. 993.

Chase, R.S. (1995): 'Women's Labour Force Participation During and After Communism: A Case Study of the Czech Republic and Slovakia', Yale University, Department of Economics, New Haven, mimeo.

Clark, K. and Summers, L. (1982): 'Labor Force Participation: Timing and Persistence,' NBER Working Paper No. 977, September.

Commander, S. and Dhar, S. (1996): 'Polish Enterprises during the Transition', paper presented at the workshop on 'Unemployment, Restructuring, and the Labour Market in Eastern Europe and Russia', World Bank/EDI, 6 May 1996, Washington, DC.

Commander, S. and McHale, J. (1995): 'Labor Markets in the Transition in East Europe and Russia: A Review of Experience', background paper for the World Bank World Development Report, Washington, DC.

Commander, S. and Schankerman, M. (1997): 'Enterprise Restructuring and Social Benefits', EBRD Working Paper No. 22, April.

Commander, S., Kölló, J. and Ugaz, C. (1994): 'Firm Behavior and the Labour Market in the Hungarian Transition', Policy Research Working Paper No. 1373, World Bank, Washington, DC.

Coricelli, F, Dabrowski, M. and Kosterna, U. (1996): *Fiscal Policy in Transition*, Economic Policy Initiative Report No. 3, London, CEPR-IEWS.

Davis, S. and Haltiwanger, J. (1993): 'Gross Job Creation, Gross Job Destruction and Job Reallocation', *Quarterly Journal of Economics* 107.

Dewatripont, M. and Roland, G. (1992): 'The Virtues of Gradualism and Legitimacy in the Transition to a Market Economy', *Economic Journal* 102.

Dixit, A. and Pindyck, R. (1994): *Investment under Uncertainty*, Princeton, Princeton University Press.

Dorenboos, R.J. (1996): 'Labour Mobility in Hungary and Poland', University of Groningen, Faculty of Spatial Sciences, unpublished.

Döhr, R. and Heilemann, U. (1996): 'The Chenery Hypothesis and Structural Change in Eastern Europe', *Economics of Transition* 4:2.

Drobnic, S. and Rus, V. (1993): 'Unemployment in Transition Economies: The Case of Slovenia', paper prepared for the conference 'Analytical Challenges in Restructuring Post-Communist Economies', ACE Research Network: Unemployment and Structural Changes in the Labour Force in the Context of Evolving Labour Market Institutions in Central and Eastern Europe, Erdőtarcsa, 14–17 May 1993.

Earle, J. and Oprescu, G. (1995): 'Unemployment, Restructuring and the Labour Market in Eastern Europe and Russia', in S. Commander and F. Coricelli (eds.), *Unemployment, Restructuring and the Labor Market in Eastern Europe and Russia*, Washington, DC, World Bank/EDI.

EBRD (1995), *Transition Report*, London, EBRD.

EBRD (1996), *Transition Report*, London, EBRD.

EC (1992): Employment Observatory Central and Eastern Europe, No. 1, European Commission, Directorate-General for Employment, Industrial Relations and Social Affairs, Brussels.

EC (1994): Employment Observatory Central and Eastern Europe, No. 6, European Commission, Directorate-General for Employment, Industrial Relations and Social Affairs, Brussels.

EC (1995): Employment Observatory Central and Eastern Europe, No. 8, European Commission, Directorate-General for Employment, Industrial Relations and Social Affairs, Brussels.

Emerson, M. (1986): '*What Model for Europe?*', Cambridge, MIT Press.

Erbenova, M. (1995): 'Regional Unemployment and Geographical Labour Mobility: a Case-study of the Czech Republic', in Scarpetta, S. and Wörgötter, A. (eds.), *The Regional Dimension of Unemployment in Transition Countries: A Challenge for Labour Market and Social Policies*, Paris, OECD.

Estrin, S. and Svejnar, J. (1996): 'Employment and Wage Determination in the Early Years of Transition', paper presented at the workshop 'Unemployment, Restructuring and the Labour Market in Eastern Europe and Russia', World Bank/EDI, Washington, DC, 7 June 1996.

Eurostat (1996): 'Enterprises in Central and Eastern Europe', ECSC-EC-EAEC, Bruxelles, Luxembourg.

Fazekas, K. and Gorzelak, G. (1995): 'Restructuring and the Labour Market in Regions dominated by Heavy Industry in Central and Eastern Europe', in *The Regional Dimensions of Unemployment in Transition Countries*, Paris, OECD/ CCET.

Filer, R, Schneider, O. and Svejnar, J. (1995): 'Wage and Non-Wage Labour Cost in the Czech Republic: The Impact of Fringe Benefits', CERGE-EI Working Paper Series No. 77, Prague.

Flanagan, R. (1993): 'Were Communists Good Human Capitalists? The Case of the Czech Republic', Stanford University, mimeo.

Flanagan, R. J. (1995a): 'Institutional Structure and Labour Market Outcomes: Western Lessons for European Countries in Transition', IMF Working Paper WP/95/63.

Flanagan, R. J. (1995b): 'Wage Structures in the Transition of the Czech Economy', IMF Working Paper WP/95/36.

Freeman, R. (1994): 'What Direction for Labour Market Institutions in Eastern and Central Europe?', in O.J. Blanchard, K.A. Froot and J.D. Sachs (eds.), *The Transition in Eastern Europe*, Vol. 2., Chicago and London, University of Chicago Press.

Godfrey, M. (1993): 'Are Hungarian Labour Costs Really so High?', ILO-Japan Project, Budapest, 1993.

Góra, M., Lehmann, H., Socha, M., and Sztanderska, U. (1996): 'Labour Market Policies in Poland', in *Lessons from Labour Market Policies in Transition Countries*, OECD Proceedings, Paris, OECD/CCET.

Gregg, P. and Wadsworth, J. (1995): 'Mind the Gap? The Changing Nature of Entry Jobs in Britain', mimeo, Centre for Economic Performance, London.

Ham, J., Svejnar, J. and Terrell, K. (1995): 'Unemployment Duration Transitional Economies: Evidence from Micro Data on Czech and Slovak Men', paper presented at the workshop on 'Unemployment, Restructuring and the Labour Market in Eastern Europe and Russia', World Bank-EDI, Budapest, 10–11 March 1995.

Havlik, P. (1996): 'Exchange Rates, Competitiveness and Labour Costs in Central and Eastern Europe', WIWW Research Report No. 231, October, Vienna.

Hinds, M. (1993): 'Policies to Overcome the Transformation Crisis: The Case of Russia', in H. Siebert (ed.), *Overcoming the Transformation Crisis: Lessons for the Successor States of the Soviet Union*, Tübingen, JCB Mohr.

Hopenhayn, H. and Rogerson, R. (1993): 'Job Turnover and Policy Evaluation: A General Equilibrium Analysis', *Journal of Political Economy* 101.

ILO (1997): 'Ethnic Minorities in Central and Eastern Europe', ILO-CCET Working Paper 19.

Jackman, R., Pissarides, C. and Savouri, S. (1990): 'Labour Market Policies and Unemployment in the OECD', *Economic Policy* 10.

Johnson, S. (1994): 'Private Business in Eastern Europe', in O.J. Blanchard, K.A. Froot and J.D. Sachs (eds.), *The Transition in Eastern Europe*, Vol. 2, Chicago and London, University of Chicago Press.

Kemeny, I. (1997): 'On Hungary's Romany Population', *Magyar Tudomany* 5 (in Hungarian).

Kertesi, G. (1994): 'The Labour Market Situation of the Gypsy Minority in Hungary', mimeo, Budapest.

Kertesi, G. and Köllő, J. (1995): 'Wages and Unemployment in Hungary 1986–94', ILO-Japan Project, ILO, Budapest.

Kertesi, G, and Köllő, J. (1997): 'Wage Inequalities in Hungary 1986–1996', Institute of Economics, Hungarian Academy of Sciences (in Hungarian).

Köllő, J. (1996): 'Employment and Wage Setting in Three Stages of Hungary's Labour Market Transition', Paper presented at the workshop on 'Unemployment, Restructuring, and the Labour Market in Eastern Europe and Russia', World Bank/EDI, Washington, DC, 6 May 1996.

Köllő, J. (1997): 'Transformation Before the Transition – Employment and Wage Setting in Hungarian Firms 1986-89', Institute of Economics, Budapest.

Köllő, J. and Nagy (1995), G.: 'Wages Before and After Unemployment in Hungary', ILO-Japan Project, ILO, Budapest.

Köllő, J. and Nagy, G. (1996): 'Earnings Gains and Losses from Insured Unemployment in Hungary', *Labour Economics* 3.

Konings, J., Lehman, H., and Schaffer, M.E. (1996): 'Job Creation and Job Destruction in a Transition Economy: Ownership, Firm Size, and Gross Job Flows in Polish Manufacturing 1988–91', *Labour Economics* 3:3.

Kőrösi, G. (1997): 'Labour Demand During Transition in Hungary (Econometric Analysis of Hungarian Firms 1986–1995)', Institute of Economics Working Paper, Hungarian Academy of Sciences.

Kornai, J. (1993): *The Socialist System*, New York: Praeger.

KSH (1993): 'Statisztikai Évkönyv', KSH, Budapest.

Kwiatkowski, E. (1996): 'Remarks on the Role of Active Labour Market Policies in Poland', Institute of Economics, University of Lodz.

Lacko, M. (1995): 'Hungarian Hidden Economy in International. Comparison: Estimation Based on Household Electricity Consumption and Currency Ratio', Institute of Economics Hungarian Academy of Sciences, mimeo.

Lankes, H. P. and Venables, A.J. (1996): 'Foreign Direct Investment in Economic Transition: The Changing Pattern of Investments', *Economics of Transition* 4:2.

Layard, R. and Nickell, S. (1986): 'Unemployment in Britain', *Economica*, 53, Supplement.

Layard, R. and Nickell, S. (1987): 'The Labour Market', in R. Layard and R. Dornbusch (eds), *The Performance of the British Economy*, Oxford, Clarendon Press.

Layard, R, R. Jackman and S. Nickell (1991): 'Unemployment', Oxford, Oxford University Press.

Lazear, E. (1990): 'Job Security Provisions and Unemployment', *Quarterly Journal of Economics* 105.

Lehmann, H. (1993): 'The Effectiveness of the Restart Programme and the Enterprise Allowance Scheme', Centre for Economic Performance Discussion Paper No. 139, April.

Lehmann, H. (1995): 'Active Labour Market Policies in the OECD and in Selected Transition Economies', Policy Research Working Paper No. 1502, World Bank.

Lehmann, H. and Schaffer, M.E. (1995): 'Productivity, Employment and Labour Demand in Polish Industry in the 1980s: Some Preliminary Results from Enterprise-Level Data', *Economics of Planning* 28:1.

Lindbeck, A. and Snower, D. (1985): 'Wage Setting, Unemployment and Insider-Outsider Relations', *American Economic Review* 76.

Ljungqvist, L. and Sargent, T.J. (1995): 'The Swedish Unemployment Experience', *European Economic Review* 39.

Lubyová, M. and van Ours, J. 1996) 'Work Incentives and Other Effects of the Transition to Social Assistance: Evidence from the Slovak Republic', paper presented at the OECD Technical Workshop on 'Long-term Unemployment and the Transition from Unemployment Benefits to Social Assistance', Vienna, 30 November–2 December 1996.

Major, I. and Voszka, É. (1996) 'Privatization and Structural Change: A Follow-Up of "High-Priority" Large Industrial Firms in Hungarian', Financial Research Inc., Budapest.

Mancellari, A, Papaganos, H. and Sanfey, P. (1996): 'Job Creation and Temporary Emigration: The Albanian Experience', *Economics of Transition* 4:2.

Micklewright, J. and Nagy, G. (1994): 'Flows to and from Insured Unemployment in Hungary', EUI Working Papers in Economics No. 41.

Munich, D., Svejnar, J. and Terrell, K. (1994): 'Regional Unemployment Dynamics and Mismatch in the Czech and Slovak Republics', paper presented at the OECD Technical Workshop on 'Regional Unemployment in Central and Eastern Europe', Vienna, 3–5 November 1994.

Nickell, S. (1986): 'Dynamic Models of Labour Demand', in O. Ashenfelter and R. Layard (eds), *Handbook of Labour Economics*, Amsterdam, North Holland.

Nickell, S. (1995): 'Labour Market Dynamics in OECD Countries', Centre for Economic Performance Discussion Paper No. 255, August.

Nickell, S. and Bell, B. (1997): 'Would Cutting Payroll Taxes on the Unskilled have a Significant Impact on Unemployment?', in D. Snower and G. De la Dehesa (eds), *Unemployment Policy: Government Options for the Labour Market*, London, CEPR.

OECD (1993): *Employment and Unemployment in Central and Eastern Europe*, Conceptual and Measurement Issues, Paris, OECD.

OECD (1995a): '*Review of the Labour Market in the Czech Republic*', Paris, OECD.

OECD (1995b): *OECD Economic Survey: Hungary*, Paris, OECD.

OECD (1995c): *Employment Outlook*, Chapter 2, Paris, OECD.

OECD (1996a): *Employment Outlook 1996*, Paris, OECD.

OECD (1996b): *Lessons from Labour Market Policies in the Transition Countries*, OECD Proceedings, Paris, OECD.

OECD (1997): *Labour Market Policies in Slovenia*, Directorate for Education Employment Labour and Social Affairs, Employment, Labor and Social Affairs Committee, OECD, Paris.

OECD, 'Short-term Economic Indicators for Central and Eastern Europe', Paris, various issues.

Orazem, P., Vodopivec, M. and Wu, R. (1995): 'Worker Displacement During the Transition: Experience from Slovenia', Policy Research Working Paper No. 1449, World Bank, April.

Pinto, B. and van Wijnbergen, S. (1995): 'Ownership and Corporate Control in Poland: Why State Firms Defied the Odds', CEPR Discussion Paper No. 1273, December.

Pohl, G., Anderson, R.E., Claessens, S. and Djankov, S. (1997): *Privatization and Restructuring in Central and Eastern Europe*, Washington, DC, World Bank.

Puhani, P.A. (1996): 'Poland on the Dole', Zentrum für Europäische Wirtschaftsforschung GmbH, Labour Economics, Human Resources and Social Policy Series, Discussion Paper No. 96-30, Mannheim.

Puhani, P., and Steiner, V. (1996): 'Public Works for Poland? Active Labour Market Policies during Transition', ZEW Discussion Paper No. 96-01.

Raiser, M. (1994) 'Ein tschechisches Wunder? Zur Rolle politikinduzierter Anreizstrukturen im Transformationsprozeß', Kiel Diskussionspaper Nr. 233, June.

Raiser, M. (1995) 'Governing the Transition to a Market Economy', *Economics of Transition* 3.

Rowthorn, R. (1995): 'Capital Formation and Unemployment', *Oxford Review of Economic Policy* 11:1.

Rutkowski, J. (1996a): 'Changes in the Wage Structure During Economic Transition in Central and Eastern Europe', Technical Paper No. 340, World Bank, Washington, DC.

Rutkowski, J. (1996b): 'High Skills Pay Off: The Changing Wage Structure During Economic Transition in Poland', *Economics of Transition* 4:1.

Sachs, J. (1993) *Poland's Jump to a Market Economy*, Cambridge: MIT Press.

Saint-Paul, G. (1996) 'Understanding Labour Market Insitution: A Political Economy Perspective' CEPR Discussion Paper No. 1438, October.

Sakova, S. (1996): 'Changes and Differences in Earnings Structures', unpublished thesis, Economics Department, Central European University, Budapest

Sargent (1978): 'Estimation of Dynamic Labour Demand Schedules under Rational Expectations', *Journal of Political Economy* 86.

Scarpetta, S. (1993): 'Spatial Variations in Unemployment in Central and Eastern Europe: Underlying Reasons and Labor Market Policy Options', in S. Scarpetta and A. Wörgötter (eds), *Regional Dimensions of Unemployment in Transition Economies*, Paris, OECD.

Scarpetta, S. (1995): 'Spatial Variations in Unemployment in Central and Eastern Europe: Underlying Reasons and Labour Market Policy Options', in *The Regional Dimensions of Unemployment in Transition Countries*, Paris, OECD/CCET.

Scarpetta, S. and Reutersward, A. (1994): 'Unemployment Benefit Systems and Active Labour Market Policies in Central and Eastern Europe: An Overview', in *Unemployment in Transition Economies: Transient or Persistent?* Paris, OECD.

Schaffer, M.E. (1995): 'Government Subsidies to Enterprises in Central and Eastern Europe: Budgetary Subsidies and Tax Arrears', in D.M. Newbery (ed.): *Tax and Benefit Reform in Central and Eastern Europe*, London, CEPR.

Siebert, H. (ed.) (1993): *Overcoming the Transformation Crisis: Lessons for the Successor States of the Soviet Union*, Tübingen, JCB Mohr.

Snower, D. (1995): 'Evaluating Unemployment Policies: What do the Underlying Theories Tell Us?', *Oxford Review of Economic Policy* 11:3.

Standing, G. and D. Vaughan-Whitehead (eds) (1995): *Minimum Wages in Central and Eastern Europe: From Protection to Destitution*, Budapest, CEU Press.

Steiner, V. and Bellmann, L. (1995): 'The East-German Wage Structure in the Transition to a Market Economy', *Labour* 9:3.

Steiner, V. and Kwiatkowski, E. (1995): 'The Polish Labour Market in Transition', Zentrum für Europäische Wirschaftsforschung GmbH, Labour Economics, Human Resources and Social Policy Series, Discussion Paper No. 96-03, Mannheim.

Terrell, K. and Munich, D. (1996): 'Evidence on the Implementation and Effectiveness of Active and Passive Labour Market Policies in the Czech Republic', in T. Boeri, H. Lehmann, and A. Wörgötter (eds), *Lessons from the Experiences of Transition Countries with Labour Market Policies*, Paris, OECD.

Terrell, K., Lubyová, M., and Strapec, M. (1995): 'An Overview of Labour Market Policies in the Slovak Republik', paper presented at the OECD Technical Workshop on 'What Can We Learn from the Experience of Transition Countries with Labour Market Policies?, Vienna, 30 November–2 December 1995.

Terrell, K., Lubyova, M., and Strapec, M. (1996): 'Evidence on the Implementation and Effectiveness of Active and Passive Labour Market Policies in the Slovak Republic', in T. Boeri, H. Lehmann and A. Wörgötter (eds.), *Lessons from the Experience of Transition Countries with Labour Market Policies*, Paris, OECD.

Uldrichova, V. (1994): 'Position of National and Ethnic Minorities in the Labour Market of the Czech Republic', mimeo, Budapest.

Varga, J. (1997): 'On Tuition Fees and Student Loans in Higher Education in Hungary', *Acta Oeconomica*, forthcoming. Also published in Hungarian in *Europa Fórum* 3, 1996.

Vecernik, J. (1995): 'Changing Earnings Distribution in the Czech Republic: Survey Evidence from 1988–94', *Economics of Transition* 3:3.

Vodopivec, M. (1995): 'The Slovenian Labour Market in Transition: Evidence from Microdata', paper presented at the OECD Technical Workshop on 'What Can We Learn From the Experience of Transition Countries with Labour Market Policies?, Vienna, 30 November–2 December 1995.

Winter-Ebmer, R. (1996): 'Wage Curve, Unemployment Duration and Compensating Differentials', *Labour Economics* 3.

Zemplínerová, A. and Stíbal, J. (1995): 'Evolution and Efficiency of Concentration–Manufacturing Industries in the Czech Economy 1989–92', *Eastern European Economics* 33.

Index

Active labour market policy (ALMP)
78–86
costs and benefits 84
cuts in 82
Czech Republic 82–4
effectiveness of 82
implementation of 84
limits 84–6
negative effects 81
post-transition 102
Age-productivity profiles 52
Agriculture, changing structure of output
and employment 73
Apprentice schools 99, 100
Austria, accessions and applications to
entry into EEC/EU 108

Balance-of-payment problems 5
Benefit cuts 77–8
Benefit systems 77
Budgetary crises 74
Bulgaria 5, 11, 27, 33
active and passive unemployment
policies 80, 85
characterizing the long-term
unemployed 23–4
educational attainment of the
workforce 26
employment protection regulation 90–1
employment rates 13, 15
minimum wage and earnings at bottom
of wage distribution 55
PPP-GDP per capita 95
social assistance and wage distribution
78
systemic dependency ratios 16

Burns–Mitchell diagrams 107, 109, 110,
115–19

Capital formation and employment growth
45
Capital stock 43–5
Central and Eastern Europe (CEE), labour
markets. *See* Labour markets
Central planning 25
Child-care facilities 10
College graduates 51
Communism, end of 1
Commuting costs 21
Consolidation efforts 74
Continuing firms 38
Contribution rates 87
CPI 47–8
CPI/PPI wedge 45
Currency devaluation 47
Cyclically-corrected employment growth
110
Cyclically-corrected unemployment rate
110
Czech Republic 4, 6, 12, 17, 20, 22, 27, 33,
34
active and passive unemployment
policies 80, 85
active labour market policy (ALMP)
82–4
age-specific enrolment rates 25
ALMP programmes 83
characterizing the long-term
unemployed 23–4
employment protection regulation 90–1
employment rates 13, 15
enrolment rates 98